Malls &
Department Stores

Chris van Uffelen

Malls &
Department Stores

BRAUN

CONTENTS

Malls & Department Stores

by Chris van Uffelen

Commerce is one of the most important areas of our communal life, and as such it presents a wide range of architectural challenges. Between the extremes of a simple corner bakery or a kiosk near the city park to a mega-mall in an undeveloped area between cities, many architectural types can be identified. The two smaller businesses illustrate some similarities that all buildings presented in this book share. For one, they are all much larger. In contrast to a bakery, but not unlike a kiosk, a department store has a large selection of various products from different manufacturers. In both of the smaller stores, the operator and occupant of the business and the property are, more or less, one and the same. The baker fashions "his" store in a way that addresses his target audience the best. In the case of a shopping center, however, the general operator is rarely also the operator of the businesses inside. The property manager outfits the building in such a way as to please the majority of his future tenants, who in turn hope to gain some of the shoppers attracted by the center as a whole. Anticipation and prognosis of design efficiency in this scenario is for this reason more abstract than in a department store. The criterion defining a department store as a spatially continuous entity in contrast to a shopping center, which is a formation enclosing spatially independent businesses, has been rendered invalid not in the least by shop-in-shop concepts now employed by department stores. Likewise, the separation between a market (groceries or specialized products) and a general store (universal range of goods) has all but disappeared; in everyday parlance the difference between a mall (a roofed linear structure that, in contrast to a passage that opens up onto a city street, is free-standing) and the common shopping center is no longer current. The breadth of offerings is also no longer a definition, for special interest malls have briskly followed in the footsteps of special interest department stores. If a multimedia electronics department store fits into this category, a supermarket specializing in groceries must by logic be included, too. Public access is an additional factor which can no longer be applied. In the fashion industry, shopping centers accessible only to retailers have existed for decades, enabling the adding of wholesale markets to the category as well.

It was so well ordered at the start... The commercial space originally directly adjoined production rooms: Today's bakery with its ovens "in the back" of the shop corresponds to this model. The spatial separation of production and distribution already began in antiquity with the open Greek agora and the closed Roman basilica. In the Middle Ages

↖↖ | **Cloth hall, Ypres, Belgium,** 13th Century: one of the largest commercial buildings of the Middle Ages
↖ | **Central market hall, Berlin, Germany,** 1886: shaped like a basilika
← | **Alfred Messel – Kaufhaus Wertheim, Berlin, Germany,** 1897–1906: urban consumption increasing

markets were often located on the ground floor of the town hall. This was often the location of specialized commerce that was specific to the region, as was the case for the Cloth Hall in Ypres. In the 19th Century, the basilica returned as the authoritative form for roofed markets. The former Les Halles built in Paris by Victor Baltard are the most famous example of this kind of architecture. Housing various vendors under one roof, markets were indeed the predecessors of shopping centers, although their product range was not universal, but concentrated mostly on victuals. Other goods were found in the passages which were also roofed and home to many merchants, but offered much more comfortably designed spaces. The department store likewise has its origins in the 19th Century, its innovation being the offering of many products from different manufacturers sold by one merchant. Paris excelled here, too: Pompous, generously glazed palace-like façades and light domes that illuminated the vast depths of the interior were the trademarks of the Grand Magasins. With various stylistic variations, these three architectural types remained the canon of large-scale commercial architecture until the middle of the 20th Century.

The appearance of commercial buildings changed drastically in the post-WWII period. The increasingly staged use of electrical light became an important attribute of department stores and large-scale glazing gave way to, with the exception of shopping windows, a closed façade. At the same time, the shopping mall made its appearance in the U.S.A., replacing the so-called retail park as an inward-oriented, weather-proof complex. Victor Gruen's Southdale in Edina near Minneapolis is considered to be the first example of mall architecture: linear, roofed-over, turned in on itself. Its commercial success is attributed to suburban sprawl, advantages of

real estate tax write-offs and high numbers of car owners. Shopping centers started acting as artificial city centers, taking on a social role in providing space for leisure activities with the necessary gastronomic amenities. For many years these economical factors continued to contribute to the mall's prospering in the competition against the dense city center. The shopping center can be developed to any size independently of any historical context – from a neighborhood center for the surrounding 3–5 km with a population of 40,000 to community, regional, super regional and, finally, a mega mall that has a reach radius of more than 165 km and more than six department stores serving as its "anchors".

The mega mall was first applied to the Canadian West Edmonton Mall, which also inspired the category of mega-multi malls. The mall was completed in three phases (1981, 1983, 1985) and has seven department stores, 800 stores, 19 movie theaters, 13 night clubs, 110 restaurants, a chapel and a hotel as well as theme parks that create a smooth transition to the nature adventure park. The anchor stores have a special importance, as they are what lures the visitors into the center. If they leave, the mall can enter a downward spiral of drawing fewer and fewer visitors and losing tenants, ending in what is known as a "dead mall". This phenomenon is more prevalent in suburbia as inner city malls, the successors of the 19th Century passage, are gaining in importance once again. The opening up of the mall to the outside is also in fashion. In designing a completely new building or in the process of restructuring, modern planning and generous glazing of the roof have reversed the postwar trend of the closed-in complex.

↑↑↑| **Victor Baltard – Forum des Halles, Paris, France,** 1853–70: demolished 1971
↑↑ | **Robert Venturi – Merbisc Mart, California City, USA,** 1968: large scale advertising
↑ | **Robert Venturi – Best Showroom, Langhorne, Pennsylvania, USA,** 1978: flourishing trade
↗ | **Foreign Office Architects (FOA) – John Lewis Department Store and Cineplex, Leicester, United Kingdom,** 2008: anchor store
→ | **Coop Himmelb(l)au – JVC New Urban Entertainment Center, Guadalajara, Mexico,** 2008: entertainment, commerce, consumption, intellectual discourse

Outs

side

Outside ↗

↑ | **Interior**
→ | **Exterior view**

NorthPark Center

Dallas

When NorthPark Center first opened in 1965, it was on the cutting edge of the evolution of shopping centers into more ambitious regional hubs. More than four decades after the opening of the original project, an expansion that doubles the size of the center is being undertaken. The L-shaped plan has become a closed square, with a department store at each corner. The lawn in the middle of the park provides a venue for a variety of activities programmed throughout the year. The expansion continues the timeless and fundamentally modern set of principles and material selection found in the original building. The scale of the interior public street of the new section stands in contrast to the old proportions, and the interior detailing found here is a bit more refined.

PROJECT FACTS

Address: 8687 North Central Expressway Suite, 1100 Dallas, Texas 75206, USA. **Client:** NorthPark Management Company. **Completion:** 2006. **Gross floor area:** 179,000 m². **Estimated visitors:** approx. 85,900 per day. **Additional functions:** movie theater, park in the middle of the center. **Lighting designer:** Candela. **Landscape architect:** Mesa Design Group. **Structural engineering:** Datum Engineers, Inc. **Architect original building:** Omniplan, formally Harrell and Hamilton Architects (1965).

←←| A court including one piece of art
←| The main court of the center
↓| Main concourse of the mall

↑ | The food court and inner atrium
← | View of one concourse from upstairs

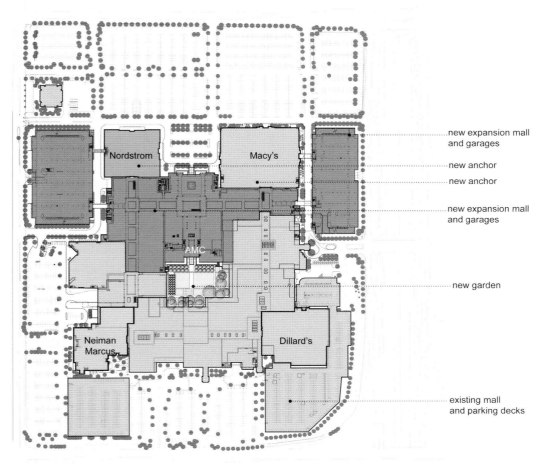

Nordstrom

Macy's

AMC

Neiman Marcus

Dillard's

new expansion mall and garages

new anchor

new anchor

new expansion mall and garages

new garden

existing mall and parking decks

← | **Floor plan**
↓ | **The CenterPark,** looking at the original part of the center

Elkus Manfredi Architects

↑ | **Pier Shops and Caesars Palace Casino**
→ | **Atrium**

The Pier Shops at Caesars
Atlantic City

The Pier Shops at Caesars is a new building on the former Million Dollar Pier opposite Caesars Palace Casino on Atlantic City's famous Boardwalk. The 274 meter-long Pier stretches into the Atlantic Ocean and houses shops and restaurants on its four floors. The interiors tell the story of the Atlantic Ocean and the New Jersey shoreline, creating a draw-through effect to a large performance space at the end of the pier. This space is open to all four retail levels from which visitors can experience a spectacular show of synchronized water and light. Thousands of square feet of signage characterize the Pier's exterior, including iconic Times Square-style roof signs.

PROJECT FACTS

Address: One Atlantic Ocean, Atlantic City, New Jersey 08401, USA. **Client:** The Gordon Group, The Taubman Company. **Period of construction:** 2004–2006. **Gross floor area:** 37,160 m². **Additional function:** performance / entertainment space. **Interiors:** Rockwell Group.

↑ | **Interior**
← | **Entrance**

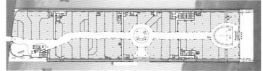

← | Atrium
↑ | Floor plan
↓ | Pier

k4architects, Vladimír Pacek

↑ | **Shopping mall**
→ | **Entrance rotunda**

Olympia Center Olomouc
Velky Tynec

With its strategic position, a wide offering and design that respects the local environment, Olympia Center Olomouc is the first shopping center of its kind in the region. Instead of the box-like building typical of the emerging shopping centers in Central Europe, the designers have created a complex reminding of a farmstead with a windmill and a corn loft that reflects the local identity, history and tradition. The interior layout is designed in the spirit of the sun and light, symbolizing a life-giving source for the local farmers.

PROJECT FACTS

Address: Olomoucka 90, Velky Tynec, Czech Republic. **Client:** AM Development CR a.s. **Period of construction:** 2003–2004. **Gross floor area:** 31,000 m². **Estimated visitors:** approx. 7,500 per day. **Concept:** T+T design bv, Netherlands.

↑ | Main entrance
← | Exterior

← | **Entrance rotunda**, roofing
↑ | **Sketch**, bird's eye view
↓ | **Sketch**, square

HYDEA srl

↑ | **Eastern entrance**
↓ | **Elevation**

→ | **General view with Sieve stream**

McArthur Glen Barberino Designer Outlet

The aim of the project was to recreate Tuscan architectural atmosphere. The architectural design focuses on some main archetypes of rural, military and urban buildings of the Mugello region. The materials used in the traditional Tuscan building practice were selected for the outlet, favoring decorative plastering, terracotta cladding and sandstone and traditional tiled roofs. The pedestrian promenade is organized in two different routes along the Sieve stream. The two sides of the stream are connected by four wooden footbridges, the central one of which is large enough to appear as a little square above the river.

PROJECT FACTS

Address: Via Antonio Meucci, 50031 Barberino di Mugello (Florence), Italy. **Client:** BMG BARBERINO S.r.l. **Period of construction:** 2004–2006. **Gross floor area:** 25,000 m². **Estimated visitors:** max. 50,000 per day. **Additional functions:** offices, parking. **Designers:** Paolo Giustiniani, Andrey Perekhodtsev. **Structural systems:** A&I Progetti Srl. **Technical systems:** M&E Srl.

↑ | **Western square and portico**
← | **Central square**
↗ | **Western square,** detail of the portico colonnade
→ | **General perspective view**

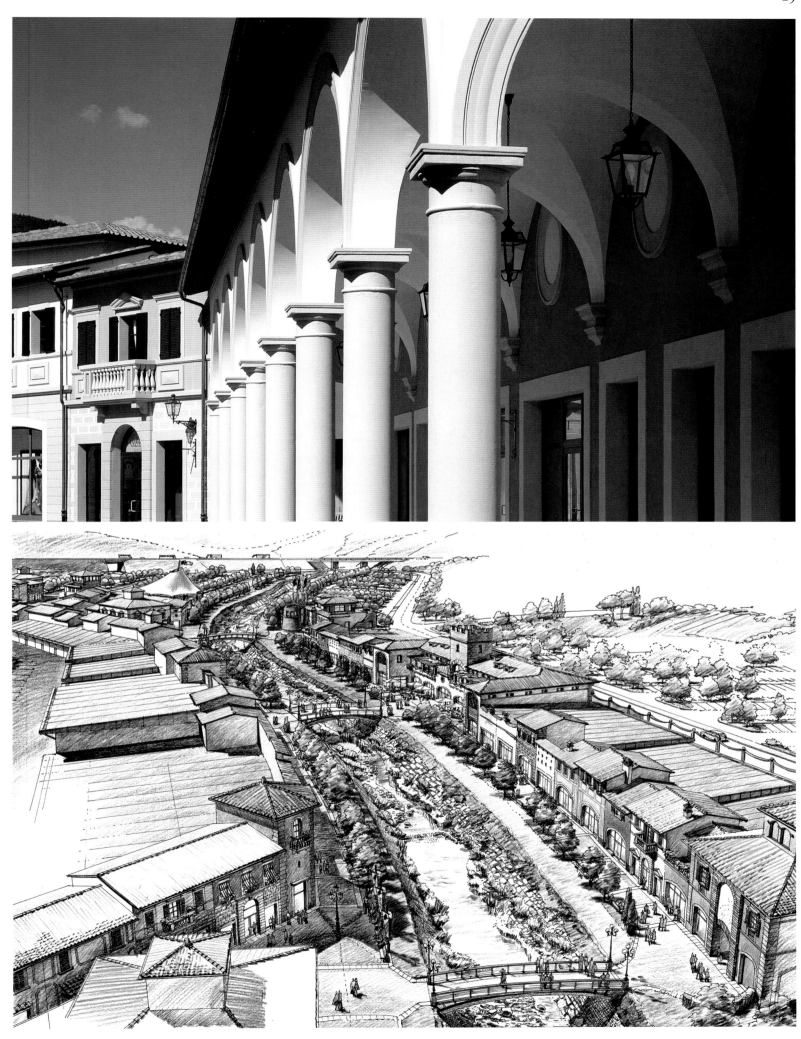

Studio Daniel Libeskind,
Burckhardt & Partner

↑ | **Plaza**

WESTside

Bern

At the edge of Bern city limits, the center traversing a highway will become a gate to the Swiss capital. In addition to the 70 shops, 20 restaurants and bars, hotel, multiplex cinema, fun bath with wellness center and housing, this mixed-use program radically reinvents the concept of shopping, entertainment and living. At the heart of the new building will be the high mall with varying lighting resolutions, but many other functions will be brought together in the ensemble. A new urban center will be created, uniting many aspects of public and private life. Correspondingly, the architecture will also be sectioned according to the linear sequence of shops. The spatial staggering and intermediate levels contribute to the expanding inner city by offering it space and alternative use options.

Address: Riedbachstrasse, Brünnen, Bern, Switzerland. **Client:** Genossenschaft Migros Aare. **Period of construction:** 2006–2008. **Gross floor area:** 45,500 m². **Estimated visitors:** approx. 11,500 per day. **Additional functions:** multiplex cinema, hotel and conference center, senior residence, fun bath with wellness center. **Landscape architect:** 4d AG Landschaftsarchitekten. **Structural engineering:** B+S Ingenieur AG / Moor Hauser & Partner AG. **Lighting designers:** Hefti Hess Martignoni Elektro AG.

↑ | **Atrium**
↓ | **Cinema**
↙ | **Exterior,** passing the freeway

↑ | **Street,** with multiple building façades and
varied roof forms

Wertheim Village
Wertheim

Wertheim Village, nestled within the picturesque wine-growing region of the Tauber Valley, employs a creative interpretation of the regional style of architecture. The project is designed around a fictitious account of a historic wine exposition that resulted in successive constructions, which were eventually "converted" to retail use. Multiple building façades and varied roof forms expressing the historic traditions of regional building crafts are arranged along a collection of small plazas and meandering streets. The project includes five separate areas that are spatially and thematically implied. These include larger, more formal exhibition pavilions and smaller, more intimate connecting mews and passages.

Address: Almosenberg, 97877 Wertheim, Germany. **Client:** Value Retail Management GmbH. **Period of construction:** Phase 1 completion 2005, Phase 2 completion 2006, Phase 3 under construction 2007. **Aditional functions:** tourist information. **Gross floor area:** 21,200 m². **Estimated visitors:** approx. 3,500 per day.

↑ | Entrance
↙ | Street design

↓ | Street

↖↑ | Streets
← | Entrance

← | Typical village street
↓ | Sketch

↑ | **Aerial**
↗ | **Interior,** roofing
→ | **Supermarket**

Meydan – Umraniye Retail Complex and Multiplex
Istanbul

The development is an urban center for one of the fastest growing areas in Istanbul. The building anticipates its subsequent integration into a dense inner city context through its geometry and circulation strategy. The underground car parking is a major part of this strategy, liberating substantial amount of ground floor space to be used for landscaped areas and a new urban square in the center of the scheme. All roofs have skylights that provide daylight and ventilation to the inner spaces and are covered with extensive vegetation. All the surfaces of the project that are not planted with greenery are clad or paved with earth-colored ceramic tiles that incorporate various degrees of perforation depending on the functions and uses behind them.

PROJECT FACTS

Address: Çakmak Mh. Metro Group Sok. No: 243, Ümraniye Meydan, Istanbul, Turkey. **Client:** Metro Asset Management. **Completion:** 2007. **Gross floor area:** 55,000 m². **Estimated visitors:** approx. 50,000 per day. **Landscape Architect:** GTL – Güchtel Triebswetter Landschaftsarchitekten.

↑ | View over the roofs
← | Exterior
↗ | Sections
→ | Courtyard

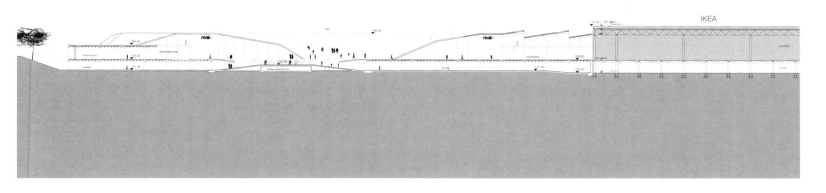

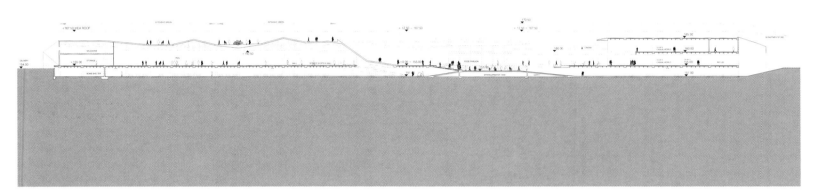

Musson Cattell Mackey
Partnership
and F+A Architecture

↑ | **Lighthouse building,** Steamworks pub
→ | **Aerial view of buildings**

The Village @ Park Royal
West Vancouver

The Village at Park Royal is Canada's first award-winning lifestyle center. This complex consists of nine distinct buildings and offers 35 unique shops. The Village is a pedestrian-friendly, upscale urban village where people can walk between shops, restaurants and outdoor spaces on a "Main Street". The architecture of the Village is designed to honor the cultural history of the West Coast and recall the turn of the century fishing villages that dotted the shores of British Columbia's coastline.

PROJECT FACTS **Address:** Southwest Park Royal Shopping Mall, West Vancouver, British Columbia, Canada. **Client:** Larco Investments Ltd. **Period of construction:** 2003–2004. **Gross floor area:** 22,760 m². **Structural engineering:** Weiler Smith Bowers. **Landscape consultant:** Durante Kruek Ltd.

↑ | Street view of The Home Depot
← | Whole Foods entrance

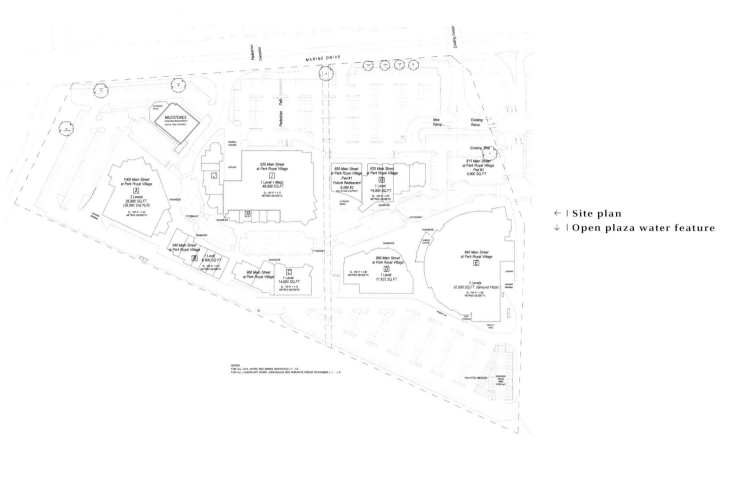

← | Site plan
↓ | Open plaza water feature

↑ | **Interior landscape: meadow**

EbiSquare

Ebikon next to Lucerne

Located in central Switzerland's Rontal near Lucerne, the large leisure park is an adventure center and mall in one, connected by a newly built stretch of highway. Behind a translucent polycarbonate façade the building is split into two volumes that stand diametrically opposed to one another. The roof landscape featuring plazas, water surfaces and a birch forest is a reflection of the figure "8"-shaped interior. A spatial continuum creates an interior landscape that the visitor can interact with. In the three typically Swiss landscapes water, grass and mountains are broadly featured and interpreted both sculpturally and through media to recreate natural phenomena in rooms that invite exploration.

Address: Schindlerareal, Ebikon next to Lucerne, Switzerland. **Client:** EbiSquare AG. **Period of construction:** 2008–2011. **Gross floor area:** 70,000 m² (public access). **Estimated visitors:** approx. 12,000 per day. **Additional functions:** bathing spa/wellness, health center, rock climbing facility, scuba diving grotto, cinema, bowling, events hall, hotel, residential units, Papiliorama / Nocturama. **Development:** NüeschDevelopment AG. **Architecture:** Voelki Partner AG. **General planning:** Burckhardt+Partner AG.

↑ | Roof landscape
↙ | Mall

↑ | Interior landscape: water
↓ | Weather situations

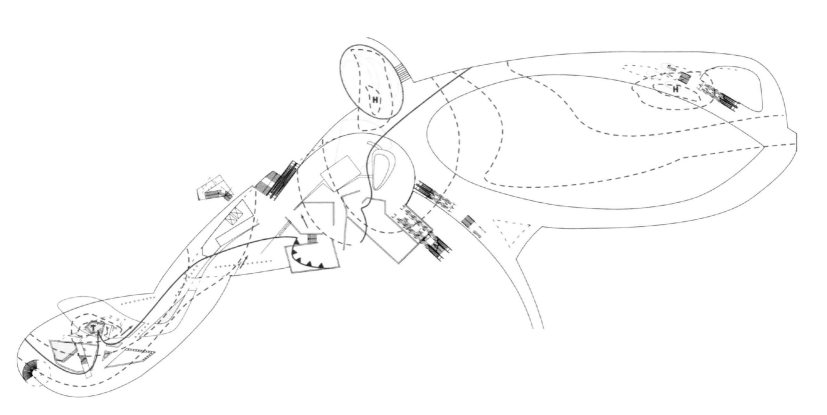

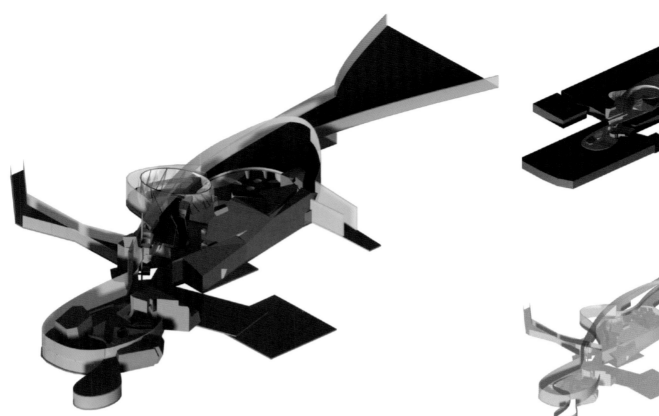

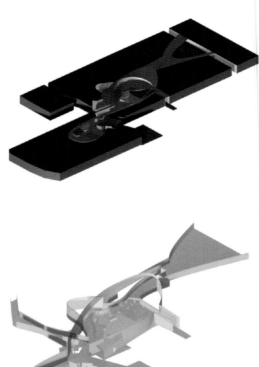

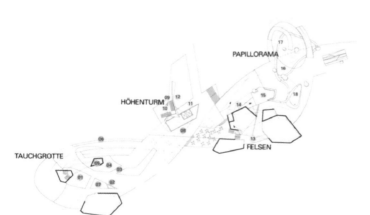

↖ | **Core attraction**
↑↑ | **Roof landscape**
↑ | **Walls of the mall**
← | **Score composed,** using 50 different sounds, light and water media to represent the presentation and organization of the multitude of events

PAPILLORAMA

HÖHENTURM

TAUCHGROTTE

FELSEN

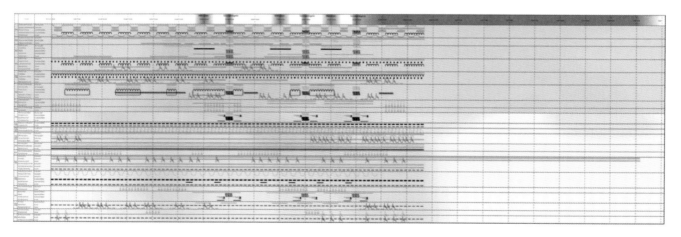

Shopfront (verglast)

Offene Shopfront

teuscher
Chocolates of Switzerland

LOUIS VUITTON

← | Shopfront meadow
↙ | Shopfront water

日本語

pierfrancesco Cravel
pfcarchitects

↑ | **Interior,** shop detail
→ | **Villamoda lounge**

Villamoda

Kuwait

The original Villamoda is a glass cube overlooking the Persian Gulf, divided inside into ten stand-alone brand-specific fashion areas for high-end luxury retailers and two multi-brand shops. Like in a bazaar the overarching design unites the common areas, while the individual style guides of the stores go into effect only behind the glass separators that define the store's space. This is a place for Kuwait's wealthy to have a unique, avant-garde and international chic shopping experience. Built in an unused dock area, additional Villamoda stores are opening in the port of Shuwaikh.

PROJECT FACTS

Address: Kuwait Free Trade Zone – Shuwaikh, Shamiya 71652, Kuwait. **Client:** Majed Al Sabah. **Completion:** 2001. **Gross floor area:** 8,000 m². **Estimated visitors:** approx. 300 per day. **Additional functions:** art gallery, depackaging shop, tailory, offices, warehouses, prayer room, health spa, business center.

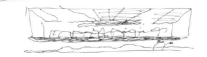

←← | **Glass cubes,** shop concept
← | **Courtillard,** contemporary Ninaret
↑ | **Villamoda concept,** sketch by Andrea Branzi
↓ | **Main entrance**

Massimilano Fuksas

↑ | **Exterior**
↗ | **Façade,** the characteristic red all-covering wave on the roof
→ | **Façade detail**

Europark
Salzburg

The all-covering wave is the main architectural motif of the mall and acts as a sign of great recall. It is a suggestive allusion to the one element that is not found in Austria, the sea. The water surface, realized in grilled metal, gives shelter to the parking places. The continuity of this element finds its counterpoint in the dynamic disposition and tension of the lower volumes, which are determined by the force of the interior empty space and are reserved for commercial activities. The shopping center is divided into two stories, two glazed volumes that are penetrated by curved shapes and islands. In the second building phase the existing shopping center and the landscape design of the surrounding area were extended.

PROJECT FACTS

Address: Europastrasse 1, 5020, Salzburg, Austria. **Client:** Spar Warenhandels AG. **Period of construction:** 1994–1997 (phase 1), 2004–2005 (phase 2). **Gross floor area:** 40,000 m² (phase 1) and approx. 32,000 m² (phase 2). **Additional functions:** theater. **Structural engineering:** Vasko & Partners (phase 1), Dipl.-Ing Herbrich (phase 2).

↑ | **Wave detail**
← | **Parking**

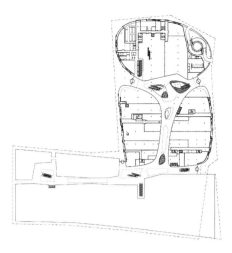

← | Aerial
↑ | Ground floor plan
↓ | Atrium

↑ | Street
→ | Details in the style of the early 20th
Centuries

Ingolstadt Village
Ingolstadt

The project is based around the founding myth of being a converted historic textile mill "discovered" in central Bavaria. The 24 unique buildings are inspired by European textile mills and industrial estates built in the late 19th and early 20th Centuries. The project's industrial character is softened by the integration of applied surface decoration. The Village maintains its industrial legibility while successfully functioning as a retail center. Enhanced by colorful, original hand-painted detailing drawn from the German decorative arts tradition of the period, Ingolstadt buildings and public spaces seek to interweave art and industry to create a shopping venue that is unique all over Europe.

PROJECT FACTS

Address: Otto-Hahn-Str. 1, 85055 Ingolstadt, Germany. **Client:** Value Retail Management GmbH. **Period of construction:** Phase 1 completion 2005, Phase 2 completion 2006. **Gross floor area:** 16,900 m². **Estimated visitors:** approx. 3,500 per day. **Additional functions:** children's play area, tourist information center.

↑ | **Street**
← | **Sketch**

← | Various façades
↓ | Elevation

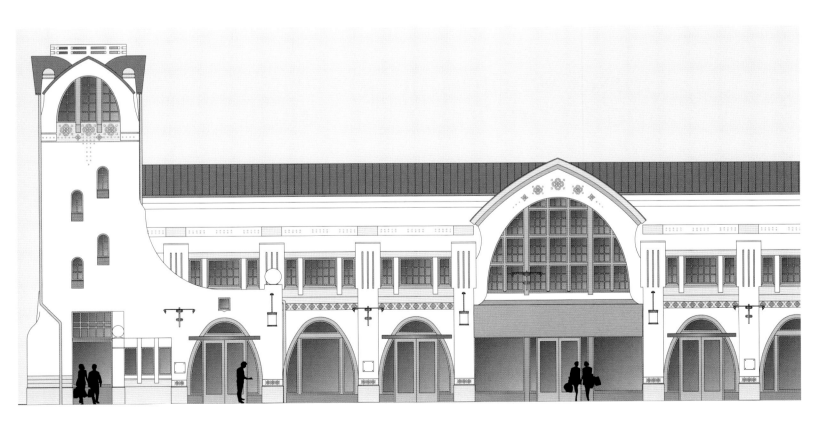

↑ | **Typical wing of the market**

Bursa wholesale greengrocer's and fishmonger's market

Bursa

Both the produce market and the fish market are modern facilities designed for wholesale trade, providing the city with a centralized control point from which quality and price of Bursa's food supply can be monitored. The buildings are of reinforced concrete with steel roof construction. Nowadays, when large market buildings are most often relegated to architecturally insignificant spaces, Bursa Wholesale revitalizes the idiom of the high, vaulted Central Asian bazaar. The naturally-ventilated and lighted spaces result in a friendly atmosphere, avoiding the hermetic enclosure of a box-like facility. The elliptical floor plan is designed to facilitate easy orientation, efficient exchange, and optimal routing.

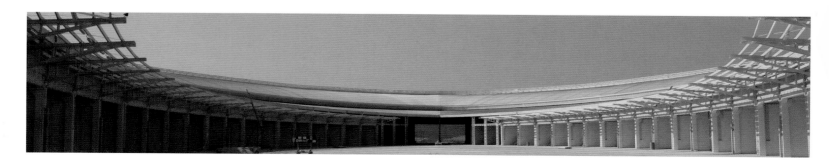

Address: Bursa-Gorukle, Turkey. **Client:** City of Bursa. **Period of construction:** 2006–2007. **Gross floor area:** 50,000 m². **Estimated visitors:** approx. 5,000 per day. **Additional functions:** offices, hotel.

↑ | Typical framing detail at entrances ↓ | Aerial

↙ | Courtyard

↑ | Interior
← | Exterior and interior elevations of the shops

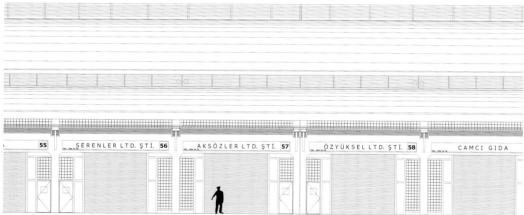

55 | ŞERENLER LTD. ŞTİ. 56 | AKSÖZLER LTD. ŞTİ. 57 | ÖZYÜKSEL LTD. ŞTİ. 58 | CAMCI GIDA

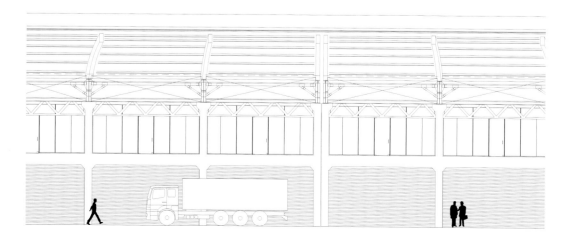

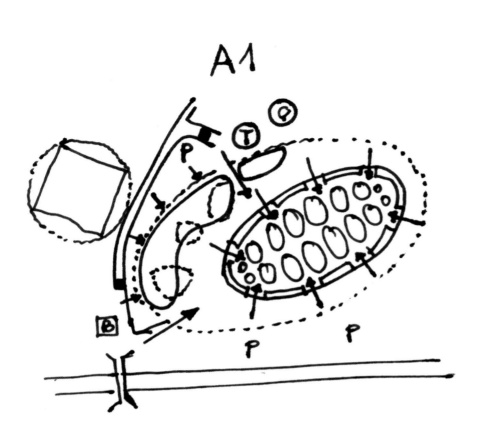

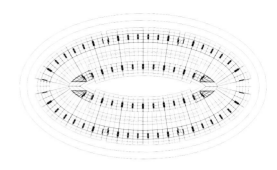

← | Sketch
↙ | Construction
↑ | Ground floor plan of the market
↓ | Elevations

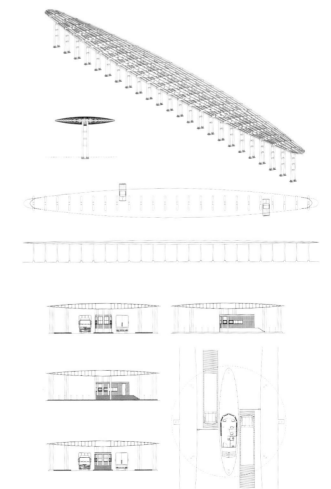

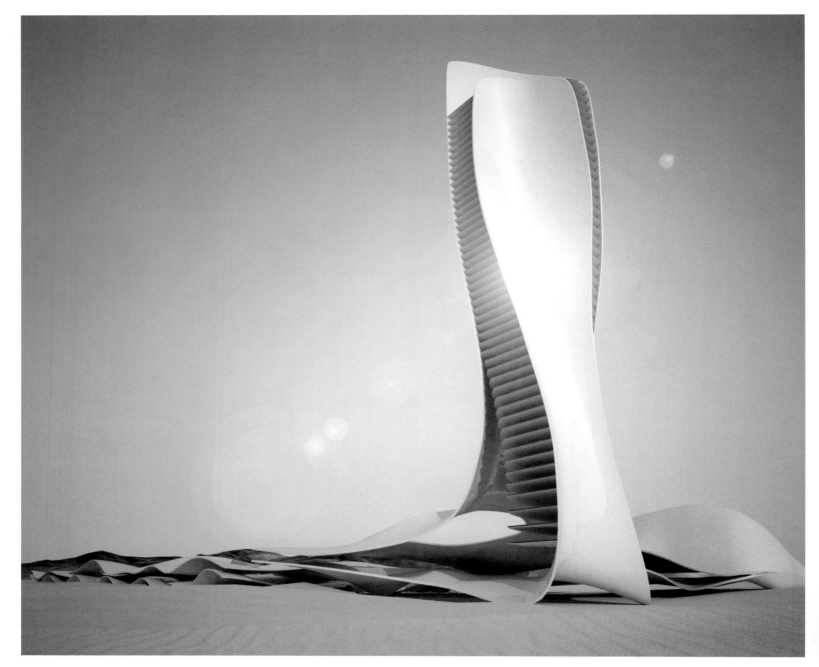

↑ | **Aerial view,** conference center and hotel
↗ | **Aerial view**
→ | **Entrance plaza**
→→| **Roofscape**

The Gateway Project

Situated in the desert, 150 km east of Dubai in the emirate of Ras Al Khaimah, this project will mark the gateway to the emirate and form the entrance to the newly planned capital city of Ras Al Khaimah. The architectural expression is inspired by the surrounding desert and mountain landscape. This concept provides for an infinite variety of naturally shaded, intimate and protected spaces, around which the multiple uses associated with the development are woven. The undulating architectural landscape is resolved in a dramatic landmark tower marking the main gateway plaza. This 200 meter-high tower will be the setting for a five-star hotel affording panoramic views across the emirate, towards the gulf and to the mountains beyond.

PROJECT FACTS

Address: RAS AL Khaimah, United Arab Emirates. **Client:** Ras al Khaimah Investment Authority and RAKEEN. **Construction start:** autumn 2007. **Gross floor area:** 270,000 m². **Additional functions:** conference center, exhibition center, hotels.

↑ | **Via Rodeo**
→ | **Galleria**

Mall of the Emirates
Dubai

The Mall of the Emirates is currently the largest shopping mall in the Middle East. It holds 450 shops on its two floors. The mall's main attraction is the Dubai Ski Resort. The 400-meter long indoor ski slope with a total area of 22,500 m² is covered with real snow year round, and can be observed through a large glass pane. This part of the building is inspired by architecture of the European Alpine region, primarily using rustic and natural materials. Other areas of the mall exhibit other styles, as for example the Milanese Galleria, which includes the largest glazed hemispherical dome in the Middle East and Galleria Vittorio Emanuele II, which imitates other Italian towns. Another section, the Moorish Arcade, has diffused light filtered through timbered fretwork offset by hammered bronze, evoking dramatic architecture of an Arab souk.

PROJECT FACTS

Address: Sheikh Zayed Road, Al Barsha, Dubai, United Arab Emirates. **Client:** MAF (Majid al Futtaim) Group. **Completion:** 2005. **Gross floor area:** 280,000 m². **Estimated visitors:** approx. 13,500 per day. **Additional functions:** indoor-ski, hotel, entertainment, cinema, theater. **Lighting design:** Francis Krahae.

↑ | **Galleria**
← | **Sketch,** galleria and center court

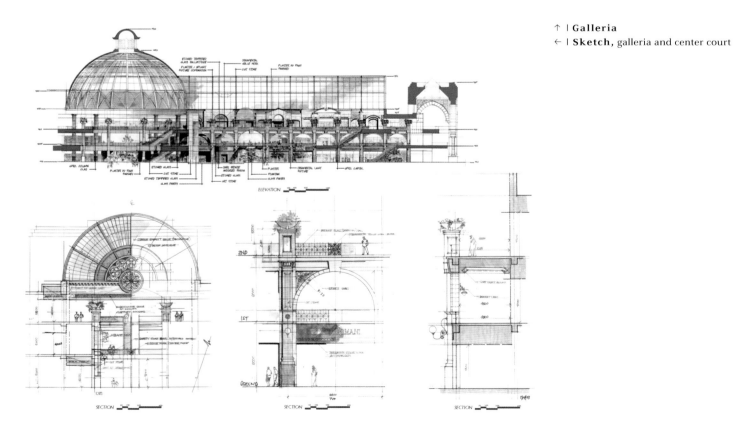

← | **Rendering,** view of Ski Dubai from hotel room
↙ | **Via Rodeo**
↑ | **West elevation**
↓ | **Ski Dubai**

↑ | **Mall**
→ | **Façade**

H₂OCIO

Rivas-Vaciamadrid

In the outskirts of Madrid, the center's primary area is a large open-plan food court with a double-curved glass elevation giving it the impression of being set on water. The lake continues under the elevation and into the interior of the food court. At the far end of the center there is a large light well encircled by columns rising to a dramatic circular roof light. The whole space is designed not only to form a meeting point, but also an important hub of vertical and horizontal circulation. These two elements are interlinked with two curved malls of primarily retail outlets with an abundance of natural light provided by the continuous glass skylights and light wells cut between the two levels of retail.

PROJECT FACTS
Address: Marie Curie 4, 28529 Rivas-Vaciamadrid, Spain. **Client:** Grupo Avantis. **Completion:** 2007.
Gross floor area: 51,600 m². **Estimated visitors:** approx. 22,700 per day. **Additional function:** parkings.
Architects: Elbio Gómez Chief Executive Spain, Mikel Barriola Managing Director.

← ← | Escalators
↙ ↙ | Crossing malls
← | Atrium
↓ | Façade

↑ | Exterior
← | Water in and outside the building refers to the name "H2OCIO"

← | Façade
↓ | Floor plan

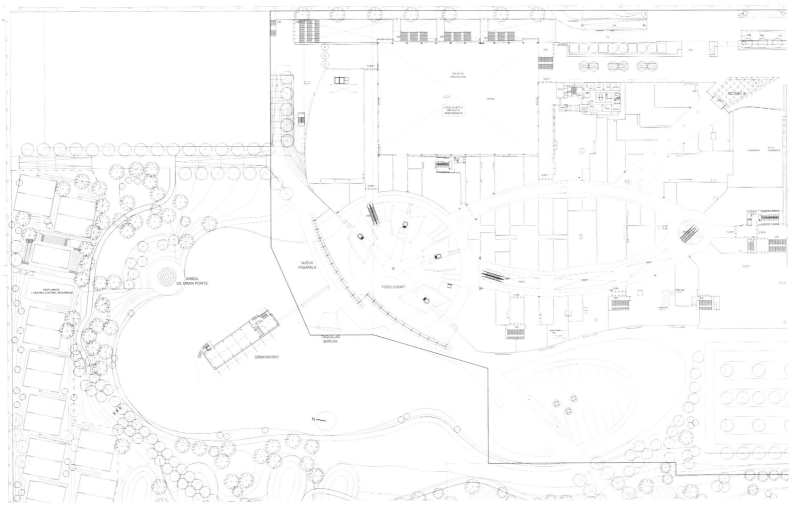

José Manuel Quintela da Fonseca

↑ | Atrium
→ | Mall

RioSul Shopping
Seixal

RioSul Shopping and Leisure Center emerged as a result of the expansion and total re-furbishment of the Continente do Seixal Shopping Center. It is a decisive contribution towards the modernization and increase in the quality of retail offering in the region. The architectural design is based on the history of Seixal and the boats typical of this region (varinos, faluas and cacilheiros). The two commercial floors of stores have natural light-ing, and the food court sports a great glazed skylight and an external seating area. The main mall skylight was executed as a wood structure resembling an inverted boat frame.

PROJECT FACTS

Address: Morada Av. Libertadores de Timor Loro Sae., Torre da Marinha, 2840-168 Seixal, Portugal.
Client: Sierra Fund / Pan European. **Period of construction:** 2004–2006. **Gross floor area:** 44,406 m².
Estimated visitors: approx. 27,500 per day. **Additional functions:** cinema, kindergarden, entertainment.
Development: Sonae Sierra.

← | Entrance
←←| Atrium
↓ | Exterior

Eric R Kuhne & Associates

↑ | **Civic Art, Rose Gallery,** totem pole
→ | **The Guild Hall,** the western Mall at Bluewater

Bluewater
Dartford

Bluewater offers visitors activities for a whole day out, with 320 quality fashion and life-style shops and 40 restaurants, cafes and bars, a 12-screen cinema and an extensive range of activities for children. It is surrounded by over 50 acres of parkland, including seven lakes and a million trees and shrubs. On arrival, visitors kunter through one of five welcome halls, inspired by a hotel lobby. Bluewater has a triangular design with a department store at each corner connected by three distinct shopping malls with retailers grouped together to appeal to different customers, so they can find all they are looking for in one mall. The malls are styled like balconied streets and topped with glass-sided dome roofs influenced by English culture, local folklore and the Kentish environment.

PROJECT FACTS

Address: Greenhithe, Kent DA9 9ST, United Kingdom. **Client:** Lend Lease. **Period of construction:** 1995–1999. **Gross floor area:** 300,000 m². **Estimated visitors:** approx. 82,500 per day. **Additional functions:** 12 screen cinemas, three leisure villages, wintergarden, water circus. **Landscape architects:** Townshend. **Structural engineer:** Waterman Structures. **Co-architects:** Benoy, BDG McColl Architects, Brooker Flynn, JPRA Architects. **Lighting architects:** Speirs and Major Associates.

↖ | **Civic Art, Star Court,** statue of the family
↑ | **Moon Court,** atrium
← | **Sun Court,** with world clock built into the floor

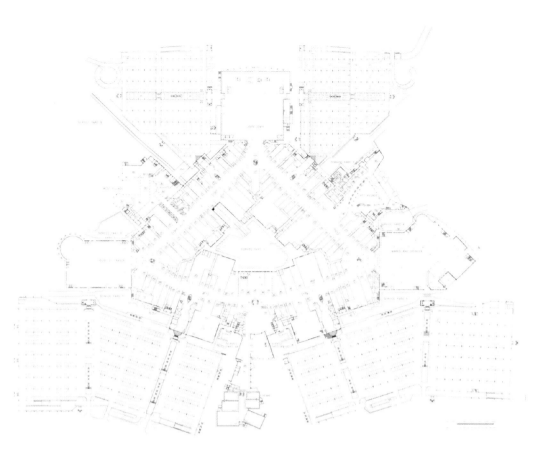

← | **Floor plan,** ground floor
↙ | **Bluewater Park,** aerial
↓ | **Town square,** the West Catering Village

↑ | **Interior**, detail
→ | **Atrium**

Plaza Norte 2

San Sebastian De Los Reyes

Situated in a prosperous suburb 19 kilometers north of Madrid, Plaza Norte 2 has become one of Madrid's most important shopping environments. The retail, non-hypermarket-based project is part of a large master plan with over 200,000 m² of commercial space. The scheme has been designed as a "race-track" retail layout on two levels, with a classically themed interior build around a central glass dome. The concept incorporates a two-level restaurant atrium situated adjacent to the cinemas. The 226 retail units are designed to provide maximum flexibility for renting occupants.

PROJECT FACTS

Address: Plaza Parque Comercial MegaPark, Nacional N-1 Salida 19, San Sebastián de los Reyes, Spain. **Client:** LSGIE. **Completion:** 2005. **Gross floor area:** 60,000 m². **Estimated visitors:** 25,000 per day. **Additional functions:** multiplex cinema, parkings. **Architects:** Elbio Gómez Chief Executive Spain, Mikel Barriola Managing Director. **Lighting Consultant:** Theo Kondos Associates.

←← | Skylight
← | Interior
↓ | Mall

↑ | **Atrium**
← | **Exterior,** north entrance

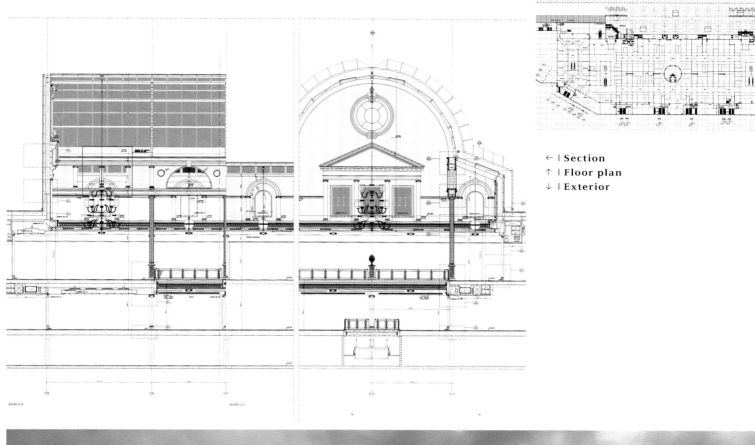

← | Section
↑ | Floor plan
↓ | Exterior

Peripheral

Peripheral

Sergei Tchoban
nps tchoban voss GbR Architekten BDA, A. M. Prasch
P. Sigl S. Tchoban E. Voss

↑ | **Main building,** view from Stadtplatz
→ | **Main building**

StadtQuartier Riem Arcaden
Munich

The new Riem Arcades complex as a whole consists of a southern shopping center with offices and residential units (nps tchoban voss GbR architects) supplemented by commercial usage space housing an office complex, hotel and leisure building (Allmann · Sattler · Wappner architects). The shopping center with its end-to-end mall passages stretches over three levels that are interconnected with escalators, customer elevators and ventilation and light spaces. A glass roof placed over the second story crowns the whole. The timeless modern architecture with aluminum steel glass façades creates a strong contrast to the neighboring parts of the building, which were consciously constructed as closed-off.

PROJECT FACTS

Address: Willy-Brandt-Platz 5, 81829 Munich, Germany. **Client:** DIFA Grundstücksges. mbH & Co. KG. **Period of construction:** 2001–2004. **Gross floor area (shopping mall):** approx. 30,000 m². **Estimated visitors:** approx. 2,650 per day. **Additional functions:** offices, apartments, hotel, parking. **Structural engineering:** Seidl & Partner.

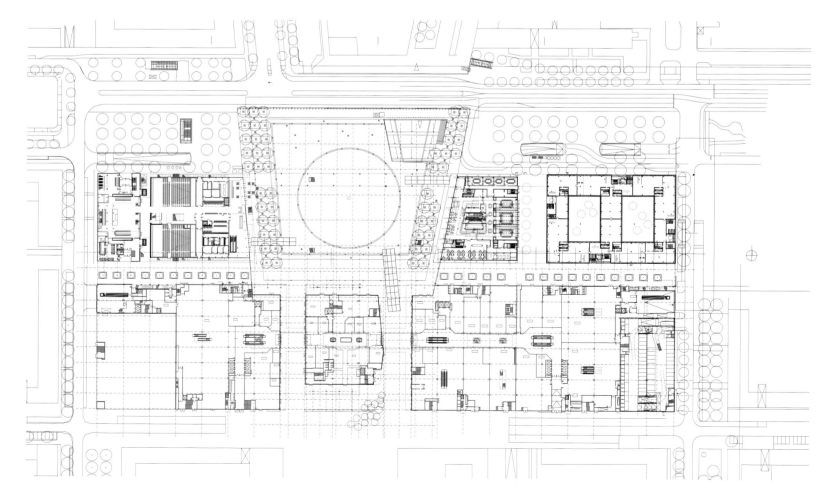

←← | **Exterior**, apartment building
↙↙ | **Ground floor plan**
← | **Exterior**, mall bridge
↓ | **Façade**

Riehle + Partner

↑ | **Façade**

→ | **Commercial building**
↙ | **Shops on the riverside of the Erms**

Outlet City Metzingen
Metzingen

The plan for Metzingen City Center II includes not just the reworking of an existing shopping mall and the Boss Factory outlet, constituting the core of the development, but also expands the complex with countless individual structures in order to revitalize a city quarter and transform it into a second city center. Scattered construction is thus brought together into a neighborhood and unarticulated space receives a city plan. The Outlet Center on 63 Reutlinger Straße acts as a gateway to the factory outlet area. The renovation of the prefabricated reinforced concrete structure from the 1970's has reordered the city plan at the city border of Metzingen. An infopoint and a restaurant on the opposite end of the area act as segue way to the old city. Behind this structure, over a dozen new buildings are strewn about in the suburban landscape to reinforce its density. Their design is dependent on the specific demands and their surroundings within the spatial program, with outer volumes and textures designed individually but using common design principles. Overarching main form, modern design and pared down materials unite the buildings into an easily-recognized group.

Address: Lindenplatz, 72555 Metzingen, Germany. **Client:** Holy AG, City of Metzingen. **Period of construction:** 1999–2007. **Gross floor area:** 34,300 m². **Estimated visitors:** 6,250 per day.

←←| Interior
← | Infopoint and Restaurant
↓ | Entrance area

↑ | Shop entrance
← | Commercial house and parking garage

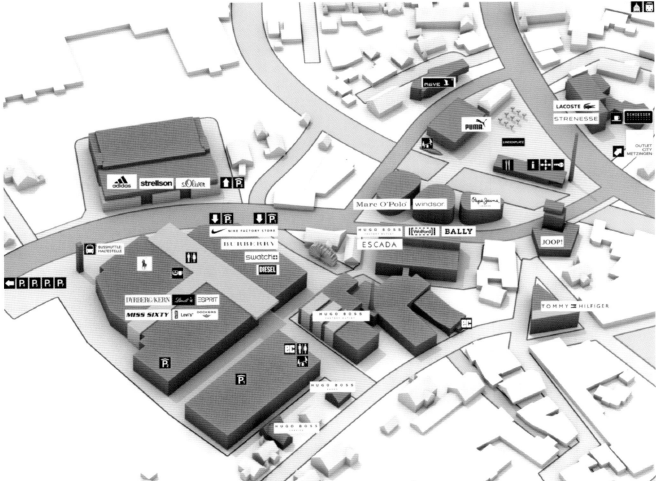

↑ | Restaurant
← | Site plan

↑ | **The open-air canyon-like pedestrian path**
→ | **Kanyon path,** lined by four levels of retail promenades

Kanyon
Istanbul

The city-within-a-city is designed to provide a stage for "urban theater" and promote inter-action among its residents and visitors. Jerde accomplished this by organizing the project as a series of districts – Entertainment Sphere, Office Plaza, Garden Court and Perform-ance Plaza – all connected by an interior street, or "canyon", that traverses the site and includes a variety of courtyards and terraces. The 25-story office building is located along a major boulevard to give it a primary presence within the city. The four levels of retail extend the full length of the site and create a podium for the residences above. The retail space has multiple entrances at different levels that knit the project together with the city at various points on the streets and to the underground subway station.

PROJECT FACTS

Address: Buyukdere Cad. No: 185 34394, Levent, Istanbul, Turkey. **Client:** Eczacibasi, Is Real Estate & Investment (IS GYO). **Completion:** 2006. **Gross floor area:** 254,500 m². **Estimated visitors:** approx. 25,000 per day. **Additional functions:** residential, entertainment, office, fitness club, multiplex cinema. **Structural engineering:** Arup. **Interior designers (residences):** Sevil Peach Gence Associates, Brigitte Weber.

↑ | **Aerial view,** Istanbul's central business district
← | **Kanyon bridges**

← | Entertainment sphere and office tower
↓ | Amphitheater

↑ | **Main entrance**
↗ | **Side door**
→ | **Atrium**

Schönbühl Center
Lucerne

Schönbühl, Switzerland's first shopping center, was rebuilt and renovated in 2006. The construction was conducted without interrupting the center's function and was completed in the space of only three months. The design improvement measures included reorganization of the visitor flow and redesign of the central light well and the mall. The intense color scheme and bright daylight that reaches the commercial floors through the newly widened skylight together create a contemporary and attractive environment. An expressive new awning in front of the main entrance brings the jutting-out building curvature together with its wide shape. The building gives an impression of a concise, urban space with strong signaling power.

PROJECT FACTS

Address: Langenstrasse 23, 6005 Lucerne, Switzerland. **Client:** Schönbühl Immobilien AG. **Period of construction:** 2006. **Gross floor area:** 6,000 m². **Estimated visitors:** approx. 5,300 per day. **Additional functions:** medical offices, offices. **Building management:** S+B Baumanagement AG. **Architect original building:** Alfed Roth (1967).

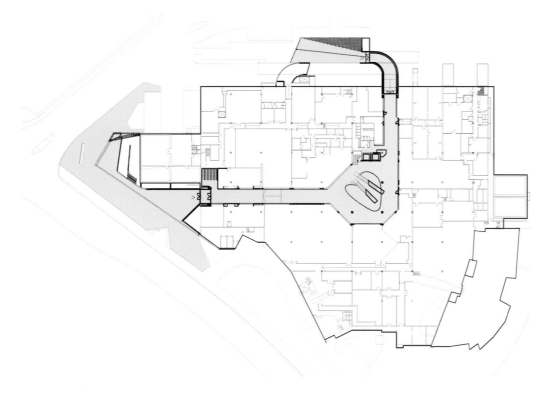

↑ | **Mall,** before (left) and after (right) the renovation
↙ | **Floor plan shopping level with entrance area**
↗ | **Porch at the main entrance**
↗↗ | **Lights**
→ | **Atrium**

Vasconi Associés
Architectes

↑ | Exterior
↗ | Façade
↓ | Central hall

Hallen am Borsigturm

Berlin

Revitalization of the Borsig industrial site, where locomotives were built starting in 1896, meant preserving its industrial and architectural past. The center re-uses a section of the former locomotive production halls and their historical brick façades. The central hall acting as the main axis of the shopping center runs north to south, and is generously planted. The other halls, both old and new, constitute the rest of the shopping center. The new elements and building parts are clearly rooted in the historic style, but approach it as industrial inspiration. Restoration, architectural rewriting, unity and modernity all fit into the successive waves formed by the "vaults" of the project.

PROJECT FACTS

Address: Berliner Straße, 13507 Berlin, Germany. **Client:** RSE Projektmanagment AG. **Period of construction:** 1997–1999. **Gross floor area:** 88,700 m². **Additional functions:** entertainment, multiplex cinemas, offices, parking.

↑ | Lamps
↓ | Sections

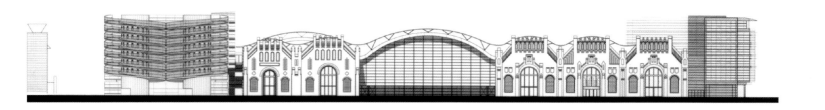

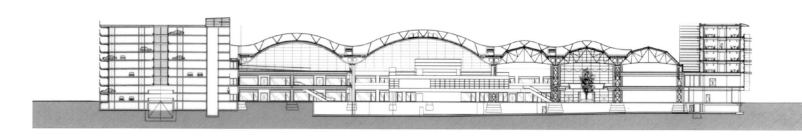

← | Entrance area
↙ | Historical brick façade
↑ | Roof design
↓ | Situation

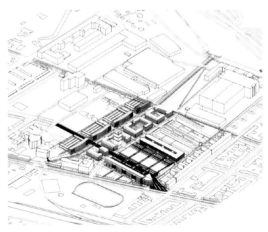

Sabri Bendimérad, architect

↑ | **Exterior**
→ | **Façade,** post office

Centre Commercial des Chaises

Saint Jean-de-la-Ruelle

In the suburbs of Orleans, a conglomeration of double-pitched shed building containing retail areas has been renovated to create a center for the dilapidated quarter of residential blocks from the 1970's. The covered gallery and much of a closed supermarket situated in the former building have been demolished to orient the shops to the street. The concept is that the new façade with a covered and illuminated frontage should act as a fluorescent box sign instead of being a neutral surface. The design with its colored and striped pattern in polycarbonate remains true to some aspects of the 1960's and 1970's pop culture, when the first buildings in this suburban area were realized.

PROJECT FACTS **Address:** 1 rue des Agates, 45 140 Saint Jean-de-la Ruelle, France. **Client:** City of Saint Jean-de-la Ruelle. **Completion:** 1996. **Gross floor area:** 650 m². **Additional functions:** post office, municipal services. **Original building:** approx. 1975.

↑ | **Façade**, detail
← | **Post office**

← | **Façades**, backside of the building
↓ | **Sketch**, details of the post office

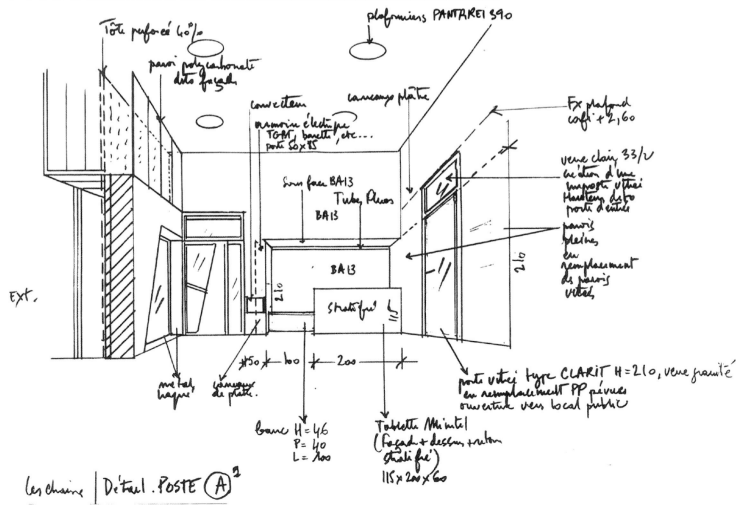

RKW Rhode Kellermann
Wawrowsky Architektur +
Städtebau

↑ | **Central restaurant**
→ | **Showroom,** in the outer ring of the building

Meilenwerk
Düsseldorf

A listed former locomotive warehouse with 30 doors has been transformed into a specialty mall for vintage car enthusiasts. The structure from 1930 has been preserved where possible, with additions in the ring hall planned as nested houses. Along the workshops and showrooms located in the outer ring, a gallery offers views inside the hall and onto pedestals that present specialty cars. The central restaurant is built to replicate the former swivel platform. The central space is roofed over with a foil cushion construction, which appears to float above the eaves of the inner ring. Existing structure and addition communicate only through this 130-meter long transparent material.

PROJECT FACTS

Address: Harffstraße 110A, 40591 Düsseldorf, Germany. **Client:** Insignium – Gebaute Marken GmbH.
Period of construction: 2005–2006. **Gross floor area:** 14,600 m².

↑ | **Roofing**
← | **Roof detail,** foil cushion construction

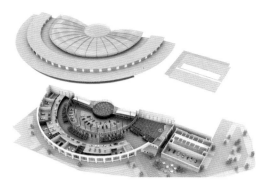

← | **Exterior**, roof detail
↑ | **Isometry**
↓ | **Central restaurant**

C. F. Møller Architects

↑ | **Southern façade**
→ | **Central square,** with connections to all levels

Field's
Copenhagen

With a shopping area the size of nine football fields and numbering 110 shops, this complex is not only the largest of its kind in Scandinavia: The mall is a complete city under one roof. Field's is designed with the emphasis on quality, simplicity and, above all, light. Daylight streams into the center through all its levels and via the multiple glass walls. The seven-meter broad thoroughfares with their many inviting squares emphasize the open and transparent nature of the complex. The carefully considered translucent glass façades appear both open and welcoming despite the introverted nature of the center.

PROJECT FACTS

Address: Arne Jacobsens Allé, 2300 Copenhagen S, Denmark. **Client:** TK-Development / Steen & Strøm. **Period of construction:** 2001–2004. **Gross floor area:** 65,000 m². **Estimated visitors:** approx. 22,000 per day. **Additional functions:** offices, fitness center, indoor playground, leisure. **Structural engineering:** NIRAS A/S. **Project manager:** MT Højgaard – Pihl Konsortiet I/S. **Landscape design:** C. F. Møller Architects. **Interior designers:** C. F. Møller Architects, Evenden + Hasskoll.

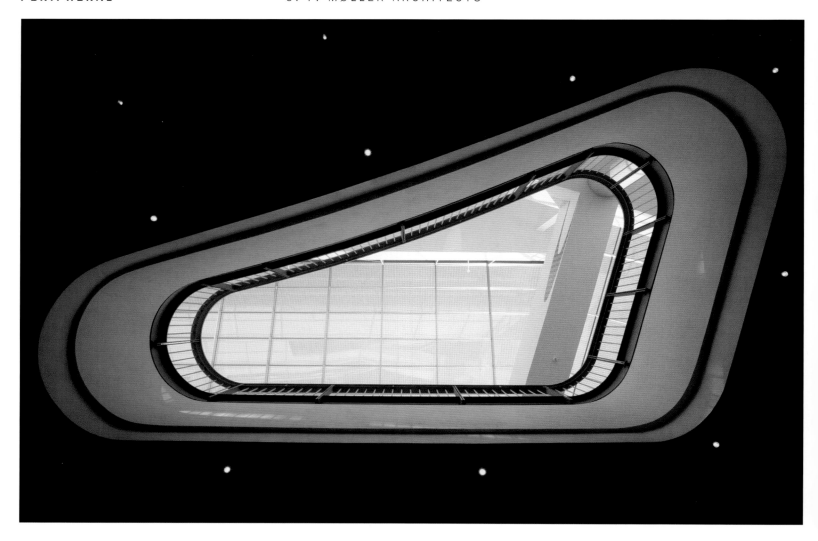

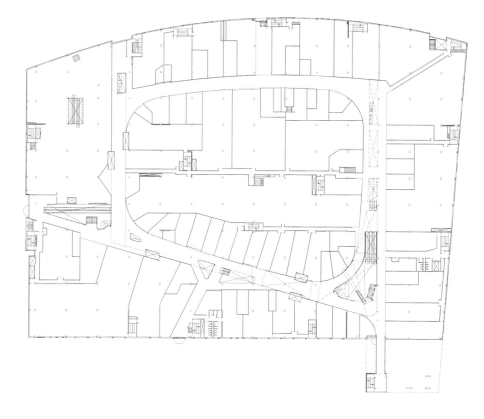

↑ | **Void between levels**
← | **First floor plan**

← | **Main entrance,** detail glass pillars
↓ | **North-east corner,** Ørestads Boulevard/Arne
Jacobsens Allé

A & D Wejchert & Partners, Architects

↑ | **Typical Entrance**
→ | **Red Mall,** Mall interior at corner

The Blanchardstown Center
Dublin

In designing the Center, advantage was taken of the drop across the site. As a result the lower ground floor meets with the higher level ground floor along a two-story mall. This arrangement allows for direct and easy access from all the parking lots to respective floors. Entrance pavilions stand out high above the car parks, inviting visitors inside. The width, height and choice of finishes contribute to a feeling of spaciousness. The Central Area with glazed arches reaching a height of 20 meters creates an atmosphere of a covered piazza. The white color based on highly reflective stainless steel and used for ceilings and column cladding acts as a background for shop fronts. These in turn create an identity of their own and add richness to the Center.

PROJECT FACTS **Address:** Coolmine, Blanchardstown, Dublin 15, Ireland. **Client:** Green Property Ltd. **Period of construction:** 1994–1996. **Gross floor area:** 122,000 m². **Estimated visitors:** approx. 5,000 per day. **Additional functions:** movie theater, oratory, offices. **Structural engineering:** Arup Consulting Engineers / Fearon O'Neill Rooney (Retail Park 1).

←← | **Central area**, barrel vaulted
↙↙ | **Blue Entrance**
↙↙ | **Retail Park**
← | **Central area**, column detail
↑ | **Section**
↓ | **Central area**, truss detail

↑ | **Passage and Plaza**
↗ | **Exterior**
→ | **Elevations**
→→| **Plaza**

Plein '40–'45

Amsterdam

The development aims to give a new impulse to the immediate surroundings of the municipal offices. By integrating the existing buildings into the new complex, the area's urban density is increased. The housing functions as a canopy and attracts attention to the commercial functions on the ground floor. The mall itself is accessed by a covered passage, which broadens twice on its way to a small covered plaza. The composition created by light, wood and glass offers a warm and natural framework for the individual stores. The pavilions on the water and along the market enhance the relationship of the area to the public space. The route through the shopping mall connects with the adjacent day market and shopping area, which firmly anchors the shopping mall in its surroundings.

PROJECT FACTS

Address: Plein '40–'45, Amsterdam, The Netherlands. **Client:** MAB 's Gravenhage. **Period of construction:** 1998–2001. **Gross floor area:** 10,000 m². **Estimated visitors:** approx. 3,000 per day. **Additional functions:** residential, parking. **Urban design / Site plan:** Bakker & Bleeker.

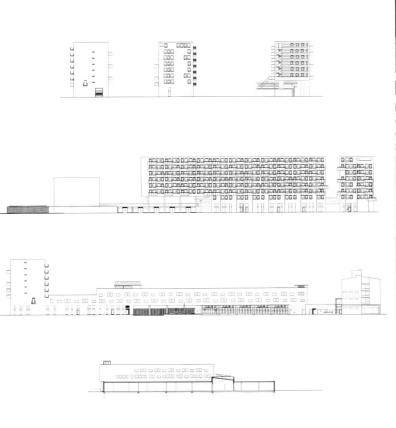

Valode & Pistre

↑ | **Restored old Paris wine warehouses,**
Cour Saint Emilion
→ | **New "warehouses"**

Bercy Village
Paris

With walls of rugged stone and pitched pan tile roofs, the old Paris wine warehouses once served the entire city. Now shops, bars and restaurants flank each side of the Cour Saint Emilion and implement new energy and life. Rigorously restored, the warehouses preserve all past alterations, revealing their evolution over time while retaining the clarity of their initial plan. New "warehouses", creating a larger scale with their increased height, are built alongside the old. From one end of the Cour Saint Emilion to the other, their folded zinc roofs echo the rhythm and geometry of the existing buildings. Steel frame, stone infill, glazing or timber weather boarding – the form and materials recall the Parisian covered market while projecting a contemporary commercial image.

PROJECT FACTS

Address: Cour Saint Emilion, Paris 12, France. **Client:** ALTAREA. **Period of construction:** 1998–2003.
Gross floor area: 21,000 m². **Estimated visitors:** approx. 20,000 per day. **Original building:** 1860.

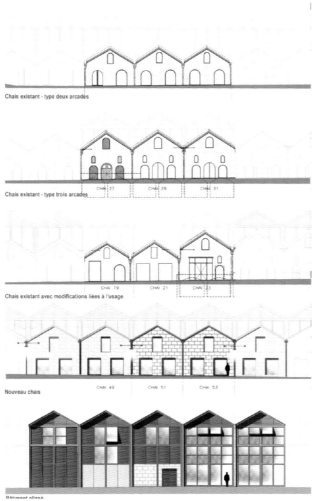

Chais existant - type deux arcades

Chais existant - type trois arcades

Chais existant avec modifications liées à l'usage

Nouveau chais

Bâtiment alisaé

←← | Cour Saint Emilion
↙ | Cinema entrance
← | All different types
↑ | Roof landscape
↓ | New "warehouse"

Chapman Taylor Architetti
Milano

↑ | **First floor gallery**
→ | **Square**

ROMAEST

Rome

Chapman Taylor was the interior designer for Italy's largest shopping development. His aim was to evoke the grandeur of classical or Gothic architecture in a thoroughly modern idiom. Special attention was given to the manipulation of light and shade in the principal mall spaces. There are two levels of retail with arching barrel vaults letting in natural lighting through slots between the dramatic buttresses. The natural palette of materials includes timber in the vaulting and in the handrails on the glass balustrades together with many-colored marble flooring. The lifts are contained by glass structures which echo the shape of the vaulting.

PROJECT FACTS

Address: via Collatina Lunghezza, Rome, Italy. **Client:** Gruppo Pam. **Period of construction:** 2003–2007. **Gross floor area:** 98,000 m². **Estimated visitors:** approx. 30,000 per day. **Concept:** Chapman Taylor LLP London – Christopher Lanksbury. **Architectural project:** Chapman Taylor Architetti Milan. **Project team:** Gerardo Sannella (leader), Emanuele Altea (architect). **Structural and systems engineering:** Master Engineering. **Lighting design:** Zumbotel. **Elevators and escalators:** Cami S.n.c Albignasego.

←← | **Escalator**, detail
← | **Escalator**
↓ | **Stairway**

HYDEA srl

↑ I **Main colonnade entrance**
↓ I **Pedestrian street**
↘ I **Two story shop and office building**

→ I **Colonnade entrance,** detail with tuff tower
on the background
↓ I **Shop façades of the main street**

McArthurGlen Castel Romano Designer Outlet

Castel Romano

Castel Romano Designer Outlet is composed by several buildings which create an urban context for more than 20,000 m² of covered surface. The architectural design was inspired by the Roman architecture like Porta Ostiense and Porta Appia with their antique walls and arches, and by the sober architecture of the castles from the Middle Age like Castel Porziano and Castel Sant'Angelo. The arch, proposed here in many different ways, together with the simple tuff façade, creates the leitmotif of the urban context along the pedestrian routes of the outlet center. This rhythmical sequence of the front-facing shops is interrupted by larger arches above the streets and by bigger, more important buildings with shop windows three times their size.

PROJECT FACTS

Address: Via del Ponte di Piscina Cupa, 64, 00128 Castel Romano (Rome), Italy. **Client:** BMG Castelro-mano Srl. **Period of construction:** 2000–2006. **Gross floor area:** 30,000 m². **Estimated visitors:** approx. 97,000 per day. **Additional functions:** offices, parking. **Designers:** Paolo Giustiniani, Andrey Perekhodt-sev, Adinolfo Lucchesi Palli. **Planning partner:** Arch. Giovanni Modica. **Technical systems:** M&E Srl.

↑ | Sketch pedestrian street
← | View of the pedestrian street from the
first level

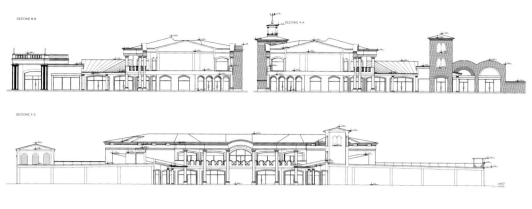

SEZIONE B-B

SEZIONE A-A

SEZIONE E-E

PIANTA DELLE COPERTURE

← | Building sections of the second phase building
↓ | View of the two story "bell tower"

↑ | **Main exterior entrance**
→ | **Grand entrance featuring the glass dome**

Principe Pio
Madrid

The rebirth of a historic transit station in a bustling area of downtown Madrid offers an exciting new way of thinking about the convergence of urban transit and retail. The project had to integrate the new modern-style retail elements with the existing, classically-styled train station to create a cohesive, singular retail environment. By moving several of the train tracks out from the station, it was then possible to enclose in glass the station canopy that had covered the old tracks and create a multi-level retail environment that preserves the station's original aesthetics while subtly infusing the newly created retail area with modern upscale flourishes.

PROJECT FACTS

Address: Paseo de la Florida, 28008 Madrid, Spain. **Client:** Riofisa, S.A. **Period of construction:** 2002–2004. **Gross floor area:** 33,731 m². **Additional functions:** major train station, multi-screen cinema. **Lighting designer:** Theo Kondos Associates. **Landscape architect:** Derek Lovejoy.

↑ | Courtyard outside the main entrance
← | Preserved train tracks below-grade

← | Multi-level retail
↑ | Site plan and connection to surround-
ing area
↓ | Retail and transit-oriented activity

↑ | **Façade**, detail

Sainbury's Superstore
London

In a former industrial area of North London characterized by an eclectic architectural mix, the supermarket needed to be sensitive to the local architecture and to match its height and rhythm. Supermarkets used to be distinctly anti-urban, providing a single story shopping floor. The architects' solution was to create a skeletal steel-framed structure that accommodates an open-plan shop floor bordered on either side by first floor ancillary accommodations. The shop, pulled back from the pavement at street level, is not only open-plan, but benefits from a total absence of visible structural support. The "ties" of the spanned lightweight roof provide the detail essential to any urban façade and a rhythmic quality particularly appropriate to the Camden setting.

PROJECT FACTS

Address: 33 Holborn, London, United Kingdom. **Client:** J Sainsbury plc. **Period of construction:** 1985–1988. **Gross floor area:** 8,400 m². **Additional functions:** residential, childcare facilities, workshops. **Designer:** Neven Sidor. **Landscape architect:** Brian Clouston & Partners. **Structural engineering:** Kenchington Little & Partners.

← | Exterior
↙ | Floor plan
↑ | Section

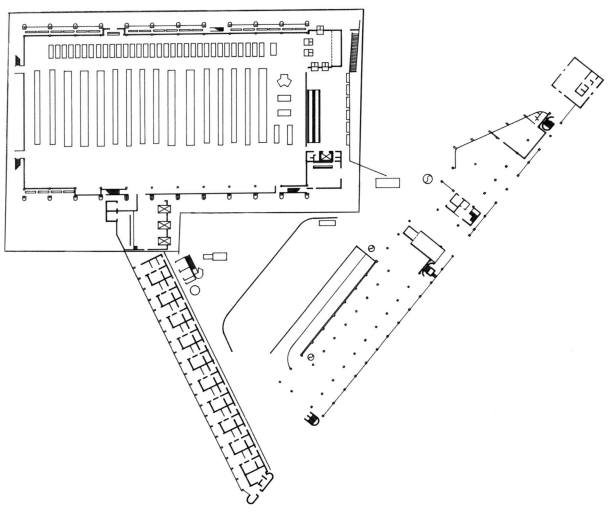

RTKL Associates Inc.

↑ | Central skylight dome
→ | Retail corridor with graphic details

Arkadia

Warsaw

The retail and entertainment center is one of the largest centers of its kind in Poland. Reflecting the regional nature of the center, the design team utilized motifs that draw from the folklore and history of Warsaw and the surrounding areas. By invoking local architectural styles in Arkadia's design, the inclusion of the graphic thematic elements became a much more organic process. Iconographic elements had to be synchronized with a lively, whimsical retail and entertainment experience. Arkadia's success lies in its innovative fusion of culture, folklore, retail and entertainment. By understanding the history of Polish commerce and culture, the architects were able to develop a center in which these elements seamlessly blend into a single experience.

PROJECT FACTS

Address: ul. Jana Pawla II 82, Warsaw, Poland. **Client:** CEFIC Polska Sp. z.o.o. **Completion:** 2004. **Gross floor area:** 39,060 m². **Estimated visitors:** approx. 49,000 per day. **Additional functions:** multi-screen cinema, bowling center. **Lighting designer:** The Lighting Practice. **Landscape architect:** Mahan Rykiel Associates, Inc.

↑ | **Food venues overlook retail activity**
← | **Exterior,** main entrance and courtyard

← | Retail corridor with graphic details
↑ | Layout and floor plan of retail center
↓ | Retail corridor

Tadao Ando Architect &
Associates

↑ | Exterior
→ | Interior

Omotesando Hills

Tokyo

The 75-year old Dojunkai Aoyama Apartments, Japan's first prototypical collective housing made of modern ivy-covered concrete construction needed renovation. Because of economic and structural reasons, it was no longer feasible to rebuild the apartment building
the way it once was. Renovation should not result in loss of memories of the city, but
should give the spirit of the Dojunkai Aoyama Apartment a new life. In order to maintain
continuity, the height of the new buildings was minimized. The new complex of six-stories
will create a 250-meter long continuous frontage along the lively avenue. New public spaces with a gentle slope continuous from Omotesando will be introduced to the complex.

Address: Omotesando, Shibuya, Tokyo, Japan. **Client:** Jingumae 4-Chome Urban Redevelopment Association. **Period of construction:** 2003–2006. **Gross floor area:** 34,062 m². **Additional functions:** residential. **Planning:** Tadao Ando Architect & Associates + Mori Building Co., Ltd.

↑ | **Exterior**
← | **Sketch,** by Tadao Ando

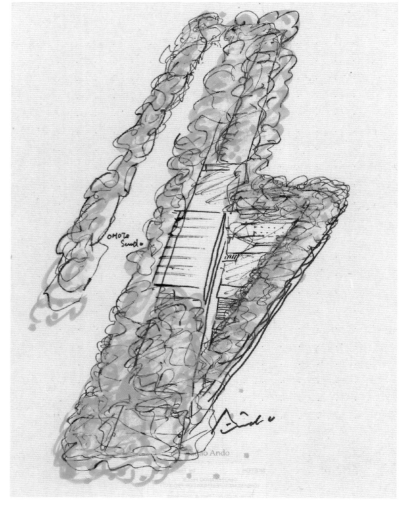

← | Aerial
↙ | Interior
↑ | Site plan
↑ | Sections

Thompson, Ventulett,
Stainback & Associates

↑ | **Creekside Plaza**
→ | **West Wing**

Triangle Town Center
Raleigh

Considering the Raleigh region's lifestyle influences — appreciation of the outdoors, sports, cultural, and social activities — the Triangle Town Center strategically integrates a community of five varied places to create one of the United States' first true hybrid centers: a mix of department store anchors, an outdoor commons featuring a street of shops and restaurants and an adjacent power center. The overall design of Triangle Town Center reflects the region's heritage with rusticated stone and trusses in series. Five distinct districts arranged as different "buildings" create a sequence of unique neighborhoods around a common feeling of "street." Triangle Town Center is fresh and fittingly unpretentious.

PROJECT FACTS

Address: 5959 Triangle Town Boulevard, Raleigh, NC 27616-3268, USA. **Client:** The Richard E. Jacobs Group. **Period of construction:** 2000–2002. **Gross floor area:** 1,200,000 m². **Estimated visitors:** approx. 40,000 per day.

↑ | **Creekside Cafe**
← | **Center Court**

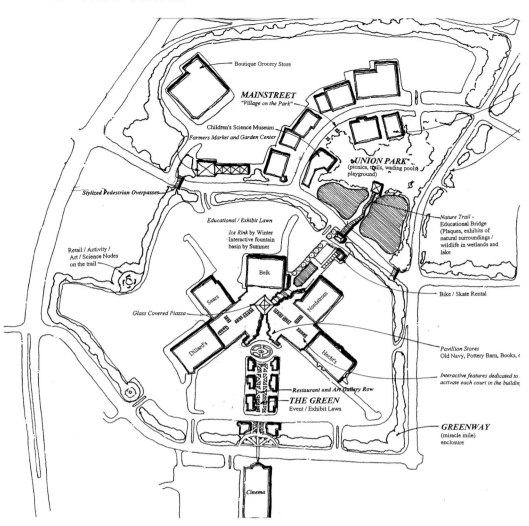

Boutique Grocery Store

MAINSTREET
"Village on the Park"

Children's Science Museum

Farmers Market and Garden Center

UNION PARK
(picnics, trails, wading pools, playground)

Stylized Pedestrian Overpasses

Educational / Exhibit Lawn

Ice Rink by Winter
Interactive fountain
basin by Summer

Nature Trail -
Educational Bridge
(Plaques, exhibits of
natural surroundings /
wildlife in wetlands and
lake)

*Retail / Activity /
Art / Science Nodes
on the trail*

Belk

Bike / Skate Rental

Sears

Glass Covered Piazza

Nordstrom

Dillard's

Pavillion Stores
Old Navy, Pottery Barn, Books,

Hecht's

*Interactive features dedicated to
activate each court in the buildin*

Restaurant and Art Gallery Row

THE GREEN
Event / Exhibit Lawn

GREENWAY
(miracle mile)
enclosure

Cinema

← | **Conceptual Masterplan**, full build out
↑ | **Sketch**, Creekside Plaza
↓ | **Entrance Plaza**

Suttle Mindlin

↑ | **Aerial view**
↗ | **Interior,** jagged walls
→ | **Atrium**

Dolce Vita
Porto

The shopping center is an elliptical, vertical atrium space that rises from below the ground to break through the roof of the building. Each of the elliptical walkways that project into the space of the atrium is a bolted, cantilever, steel-and-glass structure. Underneath these translucent glass walkways are upward-facing lights (responsible for giving the translucent glass floors a mystical shimmer) and downward-facing lights (providing adequate illumination for the floor below). At the top of this elliptical space is a "folded butterfly" ceiling of perforated metal panels that provides a gossamer effect and allows views beyond to the trusses that support the ceiling.

PROJECT FACTS

Address: Porto, Portugal. **Client:** Amorim Imobiliaria. **Period of construction:** 2003–2006. **Gross floor area:** 158,000 m². **Estimated visitors:** 33,000 per day. **Additional functions:** movie theater, condominium tower, hotel tower, exhibition hall/urban plaza, parking. **Light designer:** T Kondos Associates.

↑ | **Interior,** "folded butterfly" ceiling of perforated metal panels
← | **Assemblage of glass and lighting systems**

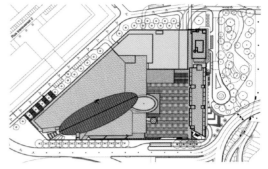

← | **Model**
↑ | **Master plan**
↓ | **Main façade,** sculpture wall with colored glass facing the stadium

Despang Architekten

↑ | **Exterior,** delivery and skateboard ramp
↗ | **Grill elements**
↗↗ | **Fillings**
→ | **Front facing neigborhood heart**

Convenience Center "Große Pranke"

Hanover

The new building replaces a convenience center built in the 1960's and whose infrastructure was rendered obsolete due to alterations in retail commerce. Discounter branches demanded standardized commercial space and normalized infrastructure, readily finding both in prefabricated homey gable-roofed houses. "Große Pranke" is a prototype of a counter-design, which can be cheaply built and maintained using the same logistics, but fits into the environment determined by modernity. Prefabricated concrete frame and fillings from frameless glass, grill elements and concrete sandwich fields are determined by material authenticity and balanced, inconspicuous forms. The high quality of all processing (roof insulation EPDM Bahn, Phoenix Resitrix) ensures expectation of a long life.

Address: Große Pranke 3, 30419 Hanover Marienwerder, Germany. **Client:** Hartmann und Wyludda Immobilien GbR. **Period of construction:** 2003–2004. **Gross floor area:** 2,150 m². **Estimated visitors:** approx. 1,500 per day. **Structural engineering:** Dr. Siegfried Burmester and Klaus Sellmann.

↑ | **Integrated tenant signatures**
↙ | **Sections**

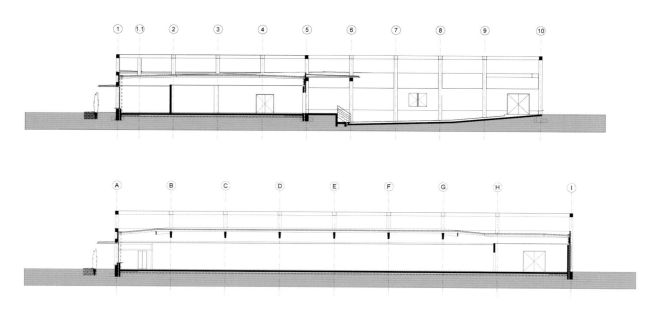

← | **Façade**, detail brise soleils
↑ | **Floor plan**
↓ | **Caddy box**

Fitch Design PTE LTD

↑ | **Exterior**
↗ | **Exterior**, detail
→ | **Interior**

Citygate
Hong Kong

Citygate was conceived as a "gateway to China." It is the first substantial development one notices after arriving at Chep Lak Kok, the new airport for Hong Kong. Citygate identity is fashioned to reflect the dramatic roofline of the buildings that PTE evident from pedestrian level, and thus provides a strong visual link between the structure and the axis of orientation. Interior finishes are colorful yet simple and of high quality; the lighting is ambient and mostly indirect, with maximum use made of natural light wherever possible. This is most evident on the "living bridge" spanning the highway; a dramatic glass structure filled with smaller retail outlets.

PROJECT FACTS
Address: Tung Chung, Hong Kong. Client: Swire Properties. Period of construction: 1999. Gross floor area: 4,000 m².

Toyo Ito & Associates,
Architects

↑ | **Exterior**
↗ | **Interior**
→ | **Atrium**

VivoCity

Singapore

In the south end of the Singapore Island, the VivoCity is the largest shopping center in Singapore and acts as a new landmark. It is located centrally on the site of 24 hectares along the shore with areas for office and residence, a cultural zone and a ferry terminal that serves as a marine front door. The layout and integration of the center were inherited from a predecessor project that was never completed. The building lying along the waterfront plays with the theme of the wave, which stretches along the walls from the roof surface up to the south terrace. The motif readily attracts the attention of the mall's target audiences.

PROJECT FACTS

Address: 1 HarbourFront Walk, Singapore. **Client:** Mapletree Investments Pte Ltd. **Period of construction:** 2004–2006. **Gross floor area:** 140,100 m². **Additional functions:** entertainment. **Collaborating architects:** Yoshie Kamijyo, Shinichi Takeuchi, DP Architects Pte Ltd. **Structural engineering:** Meinhardt Pte Ltd. **Lighting design:** L'Observatoire International.

↑ | **Façade**
← | **Exterior,** detail

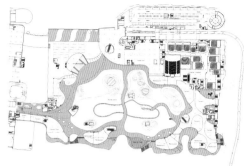

← | Roof terrace
↑ | Floor plan
↓ | Sections

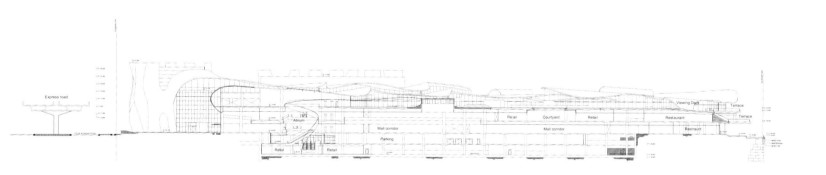

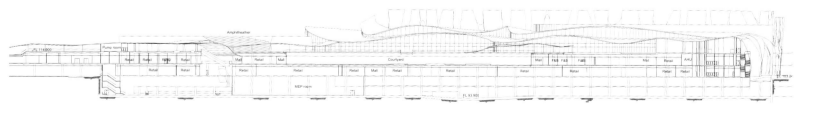

↑ | Exterior with the landmark structure
↗ | Group of buildings
→ | Façades

Zhongguancun International Shopping Mall

Beijing

Following very old Chinese traditions, the architectural concept for the development is a group of buildings that are like "stones set in the garden", creating a beautiful setting through which people can wander from one activity to another feeling pleasure and peace. The gardens themselves will provide a wide variety of environments from traditional Chinese water gardens and gardens featuring stones to modern plazas. The design of the building façades will be etched with a variety of patterns using botanical themes. There are some 20 buildings and a single, 80-meter tall structure that will be a beacon for the site seen from the major roads around it.

PROJECT FACTS

Address: Changping District, Beijing, China. **Client:** Zhongguancun International Shopping Mall Investment Co. **Period of construction:** not constructed. **Gross floor area:** 780,170 m². **Additional functions:** hotel, entertainment facilities, bus station. **Construction documents:** China Architecture Design & Research Group.

←← | **Sketch**, interior
↙↙ | **Sketch**, exterior
← | **Aerial**
↓ | **Floor plans**

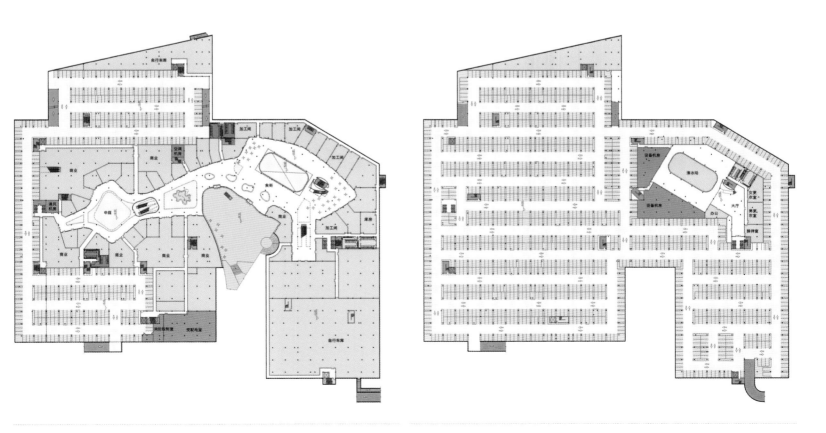

Léon Wohlhage Wernik
Architekten

↑ | Civic forum
→ | Atrium

SchwabenGalerie – City Center
Stuttgart

Until now, Vaihingen's historical center encircled fenced-in premises of a brewery. With
the industry's move away from the city, a space was created for a public community center. Instead of building a closed-off, climate-controlled world, a European city quarter with
plazas and alleys was constructed. The heart of the project is an atrium, a winter-season
contrast and an extension of the bordering main square. The light reaches into the garage,
vertically opening up the structure. The riveted black and beige fiber cement plates section the façade into public areas and upper floors. Their use is continued inside, accenting
the continuity of outer and inner space.

PROJECT FACTS

Address: Hauptstraße / Vaihinger Markt, 70563 Stuttgart, Germany. **Client:** Häussler Gruppe. **Period of construction:** 2001–2004. **Gross floor area:** 103,000 m². **Estimated visitors:** approx. 15,000 per day. **Additional functions:** civic forum, office, public spaces, hotel. **Structural engineering:** Deufel Ingenieurgesellschaft mbH. **Landscape architect:** Gesswein, Henkel + Partner. **Light designer:** LichtVision GmbH.

←← | Portico
↙↙ | Entrance to the atrium
← | Exterior
↓ | The new town hall square

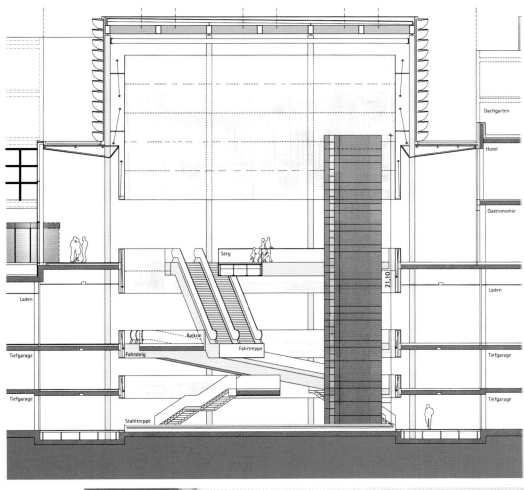

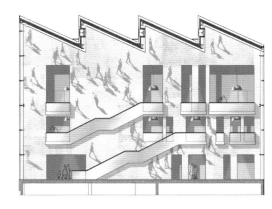

←← | **Market hall**
↙↙ | **Atrium**
← **Section**, atrium
↑ **Wall painting**, entrance civic forum
↓ **Underground parking**, with natural lighting

↑ | **Entrance**
↗ | **Façade**
→ | **Interior**

Sainsbury's Local
London

The Sainsbury's store at the Greenwich Peninsula is the world's first low-energy super-market building. It is the first to achieve the maximum score of 31 points under the Building Research Establishment Environmental Assessment Method (BREEAM), giving its an "excellent" rating. The building uses half of the energy required to operate a standard store. Key features of the scheme include a northern sales area with underfloor heating, cooling and passive ventilation. Externally, the building envelope is insulated by earth sheltering, integrating the building with its environment. Extensive use is made of unfinished natural and recycled materials, all helping to minimize the use of oil-based finishes and the associated release of volatile organic compounds into the environment.

Address: 55 Bugsby's Wy, London, SE10 0QJ, United Kingdom. **Client:** J Sainsbury plc. **Completion:** 1999.

↑ | Roofs
← | Aerial

← | Exterior
↙ | Building plan
↓ | Roof plan

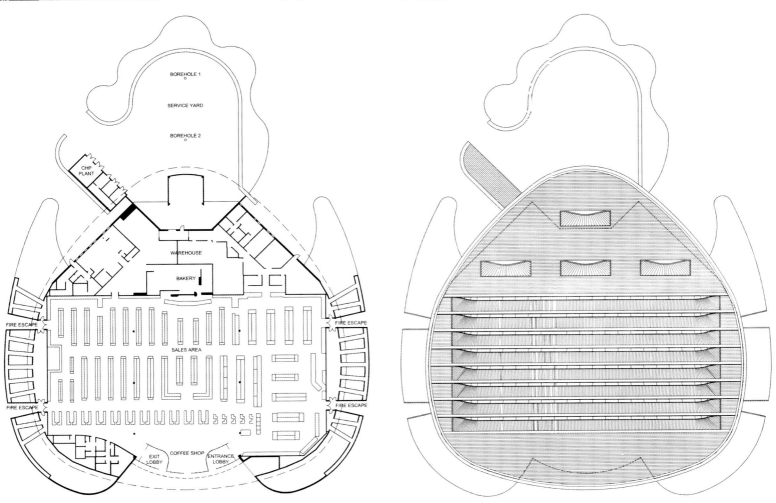

↑ | **Exterior**
→ | **Interior**

El Muelle de Santa Catalina
Las Palmas de Gran Canaria

Situated next to the old port of Las Palmas, this leisure and retail development has an exceptional location. The design maximizes both the sea and city views with an external terraced restaurant section and an internal retail mall. The mix of environments and uses results in a year-round facility for both residents and tourists. The retail is internal and located around half of the circular-route mall – the other half runs externally to access the terraces.

PROJECT FACTS

Address: Muelle de Santa Catalina, Las Palmas de Gran Canaria, Spain. **Client:** Rifisa. S.A and Invercartera. **Completion:** 2003. **Gross floor area:** 90,000 m². **Estimated visitors:** approx. 20,500 per day. **Additional function:** 12 cinemas. **Architects:** Elbio Gómez Chief Executive Spain, Mikel Barriola Managing Director.

↑ | **Mall**
← | **View to the external staircases**

← | Interior
↓ | Restaurant

NÄGELIARCHITEKTEN
architectural office

↑ | **Roof detail**
→ | **Exterior**

Offices and shopping center

Hamburg

The new building and its surrounding structures create a small-scale, balanced ensemble that is reminiscent of traditional market squares and which successfully figures within the city plan of the Welligsbüttel quarter in Hamburg. The new complex with four finger-like buildings each consisting of two conoid sections fills out the contingencies of the existing plot, which is delimited by straight and curved lines, uniting it into a cohesive, architectonic-sculptural whole. By "cleaning up" the existing cut of the plot, the building nonetheless does not obscure it. The stripe-shaped clinker frame stretches itself like skin around the building, visually uniting its complex geometry.

PROJECT FACTS
Address: Marktplatz Wellingsbüttel, 22049 Hamburg, Germany. **Client:** 1. API Alster Projekt Investitions-
& Beteiligungsgesellschaft mbH + Co.KG. **Period of construction:** 2006–2007. **Gross floor area:** 4,000 m².
Additional functions: medical offices, offices, parking.

↑ | Part of the building
← | Construction details roof
↗ | Sections
→ | Façade

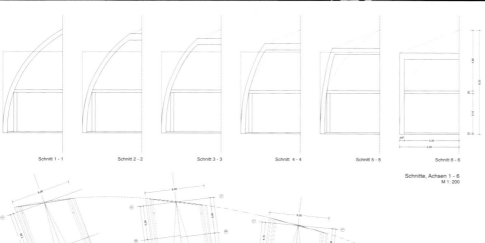

Schnitt 1 - 1   Schnitt 2 - 2   Schnitt 3 - 3   Schnitt 4 - 4   Schnitt 5 - 5   Schnitt 6 - 6

Schnitte, Achsen 1 - 6
M 1 : 200

Grundriss 1.OG - Darstellung der
Konstruktionsachsen
M 1 : 200

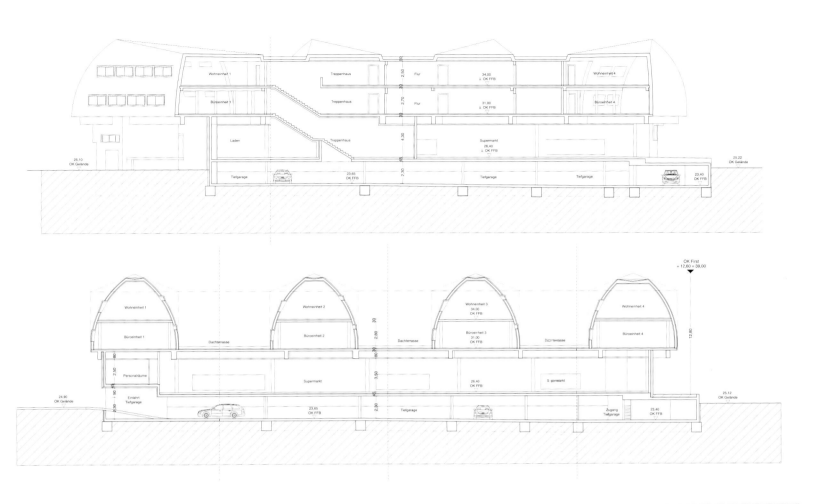

José Manuel Quintela da Fonseca

↑ | Façade
→ | Mall

Centro Vasco da Gama

Lisbon

The Centro Comercial Galerias Monumental is Iberean peninsula's biggest shopping center and one of the biggest in all of Europe. It originated in what was the main entrance hall (the sun door) of the Expo 1998, whose intentions included the creation of a second city center. The sale of each building for post-Expo use was closed in advance, ensuring that the site would not be abandoned after the event. The planned redevelopment presented the city with a generous mall with a giant glass dome.

PROJECT FACTS

Address: Av. D. João II, Lote 1.05.02, 1990 – 094 Lisbon, Portugal. **Client:** Sonae Sierra / ING Real Estate. **Completion:** 1999. **Gross floor area:** 47,702 m². **Estimated visitors:** approx. 64,000 per day. **Additional functions:** 10 cinema screenplays, health club, kindergarden. **Developer:** Sonae Sierra / ING Real Estate. **Original building:** Daciano Costa.

↑ | **Glass roof,** sunshine
← | **Lavatory**

← ❘ **Glass roof**, rainy weather
↓ ❘ **Mall**

Helin & Co Architects

↑ | **Light traffic lane to the terminal**
→ | **Solakäytävä gallery**

Sello Commercial Center

Espoo

The building with several glass-roofed openings and various views encourages the perception of the gallery space as a whole. The variety of interior materials has been carefully selected. The main themes were durability, elegance, warmth and light tones. The façade structures are light weight elements stiffened with steel studs, or so-called thermo purlin structures, as well as glass brick, steel-glass and aluminum glass elements. There are several glass roofs in the shopping center, the largest one of which measures 25 x 31 meters and covers the central lobby in the second construction stage. The large glass roofs are built on steel lattices implementing tension and compression rods.

PROJECT FACTS

Address: Leppävaarankatu 3–11, Espoo, Finland. **Client:** Real estate limited Kiinteistö Oy Kauppakeskus Sello, City of Espoo. **Completion:** 2005. **Gross floor area:** 170,330 m². **Estimated visitors:** approx. 50,000 per day. **Additional functions:** regional library, chamber music hall and school, offices, housing. **Project team:** Pekka Helin, Jutta Haarti-Katajainen, Tuomas Wichmann, Harri Koski, Hanna Euro. **Structural Engineering:** Finnmap Consulting Oy. **Lighting design:** JP Building Engineering Ltd / Marjatta von Schoultz.

↑ | **Sellonaukio inner square,** escalators
← | **Steel and glass canopy over Alberga promenade,** the light traffic lane to the terminal

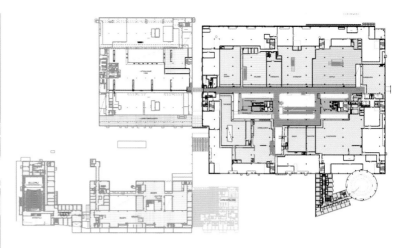

← | **Sellonaukio inner square,** winding stairs
↙ | **Steel support of the escalator**
↑ | **Floor plan**
↓ | **Ratsusola,** light traffic lane

↑ | **Entrance**
→ | **Façade**

Dolce Vita Coimbra

Coimbra

The retail center is an example of integrated planning. The main façade is defined by a glass rotunda, while the arched back wall leans onto the curve of the stadium. The commercial use of the area around the stadium finances the sports complex, which its shares the infrastructure with the shops. A fly-over connects the front to a new recreation center, a multiuse pavilion, and 202 residential units. Two levels are completely below ground, which prevented any direct natural light from reaching them, an issue that played an important role in the project. The glass façade and the cemented steel frame create a contrast to the stone sections, which protect the upper floors from excess direct sunlight.

PROJECT FACTS

Address: Rua General Humberto Delgado 207–211, Coimbra, Portugal. **Client**: Chamartín Imobiliára.
Period of contruction: 2003–2005. **Gross floor area**: 61,665 m². **Additional functions**: movie theater, play
center. **Planning partner**: Suttle Mindlin.

↑ | Interior
← | Floor plan

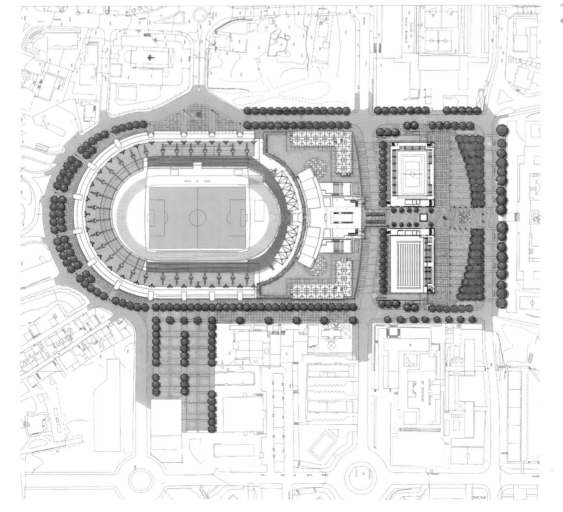

← | Restrooms
↙↓   Light impressions

Altoon + Porter Architects,
LLP

↑ | **Interior court**
↘ | **Art glass panel**

↑ | **Retail passage**
↓ | **Graphics**

Warringah Mall
Brookvale

The renovation and expansion of Warringah Mall in northern Sydney reinstated a visual clarity to the area using a concept of neighborhood series. The new design captures the beachside ambiance of the 16-hectare site, while adding two new spaces: an interior room and exterior place for public gatherings as well as 133 additional tenant spaces for a total of 272 shops. The use of unexpected iconography and the center's flexible design reflect the project's location at the confluence of three ecological zones – hillside, valley and beachfront. This diversity of climatic conditions generated a complex that is equally diverse in its architecture, ranging from enclosed and semi-enclosed spaces to a retail wing that was left completely open to the air.

PROJECT FACTS

Address: Old Pittwater Rd. and Condamine St., Brookvale, NSW, Australia. **Clients:** AMP Henderson Global Investors, Warringah Mall Pty Limited & AMP Asset Management. **Period of construction:** 1961–1963, 1995–1998. **Gross floor area:** 125,000 m². **Additional function:** cinema. **Associate architects:** Thrum Architects Pty Ltd., Woods Bagot Pty. Ltd. **Structural engineering:** Hyder Consulting Australia Pty Ltd. **Interior design:** MBBD. **Landscape architect:** Site Image.

↑ | Indoor detail
↓ | Transition rotunda

↑ | Canopy profile
↓ | Outdoor court

↑ | **MPREIS Niederndorf**
↗ | **MPREIS Niederndorf**
→ | **MPREIS Niederndorf,** façades

MPREIS branch stores
Austria

Regional, modern local distribution in Tirol is the base of the company philosophy that sees commercial viability, social responsibility and protection of natural resources as belonging together. Not only does the range of goods correspond to this ideal, but also the buildings consciously distance themselves from anonymous "discount architecture." The store branches are designed as modern architecture in cross-talk with regional style. Every market was created as a unique building for its specific location, but all MPREIS stores are easily recognizable as such. Sustainable architecture is synonymous with sustainable goods and modern architecture creates a corporate identity. The MPREIS in Niederdorf designed by Peter Lorenz using untreated barked spruce logs illustrates these qualities. Additional stores are found on following pages.

Example on this two pages: MPREIS Niederndorf by peterlorenzateliers. **Address:** Audorfer Strasse 20, 6342 Niederndorf, Austria. **Client:** MPREIS Warenvertriebs GmbH. **Completion:** 2005. **Structural engineering:** DI Alfred Brunnsteiner. **Landscape architect:** Florian Lorenz. **Artist:** Michaela Mölk-Schweeger.

WESTANSICHT

OSTANSICHT

SÜDANSICHT

NORDANSICHT

MPREIS
NIEDERNDORF
ANSICHT

↑ | **MPREIS Matrei in Osttirol** Hans-Peter Machné, 2004.
← | **MPREIS Telfs** Peter Lorenz, 2001.
↗ | **MPREIS Wattens** Dominique Perrault, 2000.
→ | **MPREIS Sölden** Raimund Rainer, 2007.
→→| **MPREIS Nauders**, Julia Fügenschuh and Christof Hrdlovics, 2005.

↑ | **MPREIS Innsbruck Innrain**, Johann Obermoser 2007.
← | **MPREIS Tannheim** Helmut Seelos, 2006.
→ | **MPREIS Innsbruck Bahnhof**, Rainer Köberl, 2004.

Dowr

Downtown

town

↑ | **Exterior,** curved site
→ | **Escalators**

Selfridges Birmingham

Birmingham

Selfridges required a state-of-the-art department store that would provide an architectural landmark for Birmingham. The building became a genuine catalyst for urban regeneration in Birmingham and has set a standard to the future development of the Digbeth area. The form of the building is soft and curvaceous in response to the natural shape of the site, wrapping over the top to form the roof. The skin of anodized aluminum discs uses conventional rain screen techniques; innovation comes through aesthetics, not technology. Large abstract glazed areas for shop windows and views in and out of restaurants and offices are carved out of the overall form. The fluidity of the building's form is matched inside with an organically shaped atrium stretching across the floor plan.

PROJECT FACTS

Address: Upper Mall East, Bullring, Birmingham B5 4BP, United Kingdom. **Client:** Selfridges & Co. **Completion:** 2003. **Gross floor area:** 25,000 m². **Structural and services engineering:** Arup. **Quantity surveyor:** Boyden & Co. **Contractor:** Laing O'Rourke.

↑ | **Façade,** balconies
← | **Sketch**

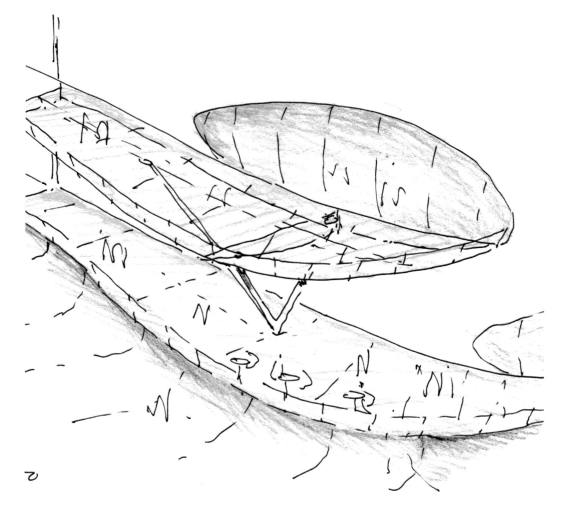

← | **Bridge**, leading into the building
↑ | **Sketch**, bridge
↓ | **City skyline at night**

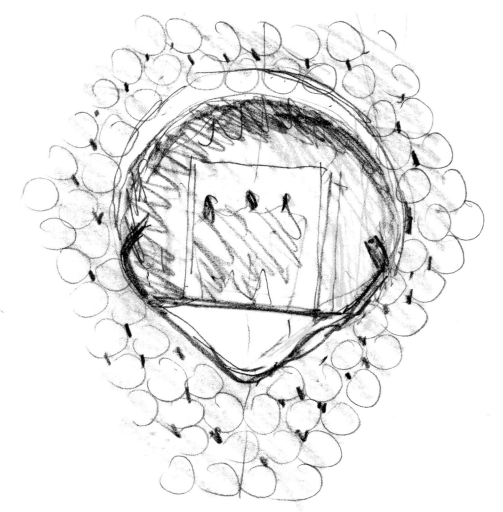

←− | **Atrium**
← | **Sketch**
↑ | **Royal Mail stamp**
↓ | **Interior,** detail skylight

↑ | Exterior
↗ | Façades
→ | Crossing streets

De Citadel

Almere

Located at the heart of the new town of Almere, the dual-purpose block designed by Christian de Portzamparc fits into Rem Koolhaas' multi-layered urban plan. The block is fragmented by the crossing of two pedestrian high streets built onto a structural plate, which accommodates the public car network and parking below ground. Above the high streets, colorful houses are distributed around a large convex meadow, preserving the intimacy of the inhabitants.

PROJECT FACTS

Address: above the Hospitaalweg - Almere State, Almere, The Netherlands. **Client:** Ontwikkelings Combinate Chappij – Almere Hart. **Period of construction:** 2000–2006. **Gross floor area:** 45,000 m². **Estimated visitors:** approx. 4,300 per day. **Additional functions:** housing, parking. **Master planner:** OMA Rem Koolhaas.

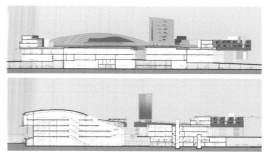

←← | **On the roof,** dwelling houses around a large convex meadow
↙↙ | **Colorful houses**
⤵ | **Aerial view**
↑ | **Sections**
↓ | **Exterior**

↑ | **Façade**
↗ | **Exterior,** by day
→ | **Exterior,** by night

Galleria Hall West
Seoul

The Galleria's transformation into a more upscale shopping center while retaining its trendy and unique appeal had to be expressed in its new façade and interior. This was accomplished using 4,330 glass discs hung on a metal substructure attached to the existing façade. The discs are treated with an iridescent foil, resulting in a constantly changing perception of the façade. At night the discs are illuminated by a dynamic reflection of the weather condition of the past day. The interior renovation is focused on the general store areas between the individual shops. The circulation spaces have been streamlined, providing "catwalks" of light-colored, glossy co-coordinated walkways and ceilings, to improve orientation and give the store a bright, fresh image.

PROJECT FACTS

Address: 515, Apgujung-dong, Kangnam-ku, Seoul 135-110, South Korea. **Client:** Hanwha Stores Company, Limited. **Period of construction:** 2003–2004. **Gross floor area:** 21,985 m² **Light design:** cooperatively with ArupLightning.

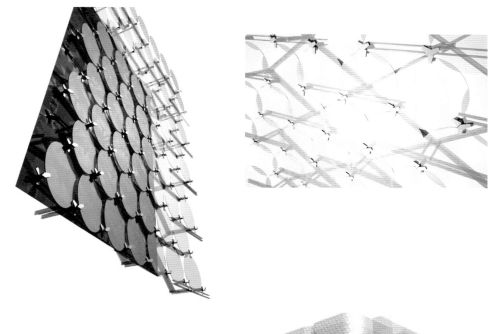

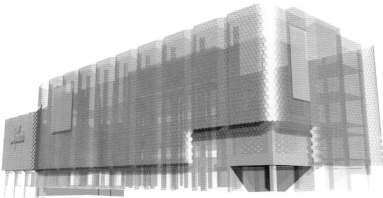

←← | **Interior**
←↖ | **Façade**, construction studies
↙ | **Façade**, color by night
↓ | **Façade**, detail

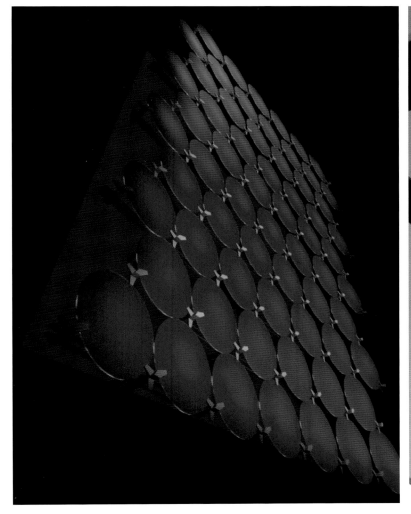

Chapman Taylor

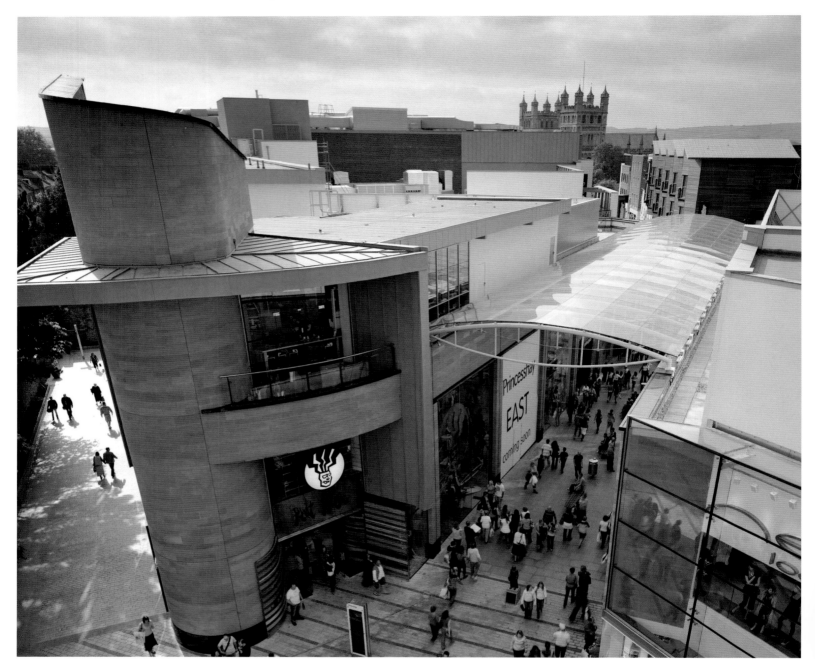

↑ | **View over the shopping center to Exeter cathedral**
→ | **Stairs**

Princesshay

Exeter

The aim of this mixed-used city center scheme is to provide a unique retail and residential city center development in the heart of Exeter's conservation 'area. It reintroduces a historic urban grain through the use of different architectural styles. Chapman Taylor is the design architect for the central part of the scheme and coordinating architect for the overall masterplan. The improvement and opening-up of vistas to the city's cathedral and the sympathetic architectural relationship with the three scheduled monuments located within the site, creates an exciting townscape in the context of the regeneration program.

Address: Princesshay, Exeter EX1 1GE, United Kingdom. **Client**: Land Securities. **Completion**: 2007. **Gross floor area**: 39,000 m². **Additional functions**: 121 residential units, tourist information center and heritage visitors' center. **Collaborating architects**: Wilkinson Eyre and Panter Hudspith. **Structural engineering**: Upton McGougan. **Landscape architect**: Livingston Eyre Associates. **Lighting designer**: BDP Lighting.

↑ | Façades
← | Roofing

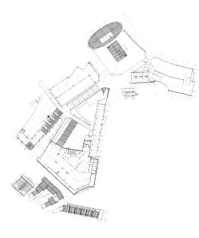

– | Residential units
‒ | Floor plan
⌐ | View over the roofs to Exeter cathedral

RKW Rhode Kellermann
Wawrowsky Architektur +
Städtebau

↑ | **Façade,** historical façade
→ | **Atrium**

Karstadt

Leipzig

The new department store was built behind the façade of the former Althoff department store. The clear vertical and horizontal structure of the old building's façades is carried forth on the one hand by freestanding oval spun concrete supports, and further defined on the other hand by the building's cornices. In accordance with the 1912 design, shop windows are shaped like bays. The wooden windows with mullions on the first four of the total of six floors were recreated according to historical designs. The concept behind this department store is brought to the standards of a mall by connecting countless small shops and implementing corresponding architectural design. Inviting entrances and broad corridors meet in a central glass-roofed light well. Because of the concave geometry of the façade of the new building on Petersstraße, the walkways had to be widened.

PROJECT FACTS

Address: Petersstraße / Neumarkt, 04109 Leipzig, Germany. **Client:** Karstadt Immobilien AG & Co. KG. **Period of construction:** 2004–2006. **Gross floor area:** 35,000 m². **Origina building:** Gustav Pflaume (1912–1914).

←| **Atrium**
—| **Exterior,** between two old parts
↙| **Skylight**

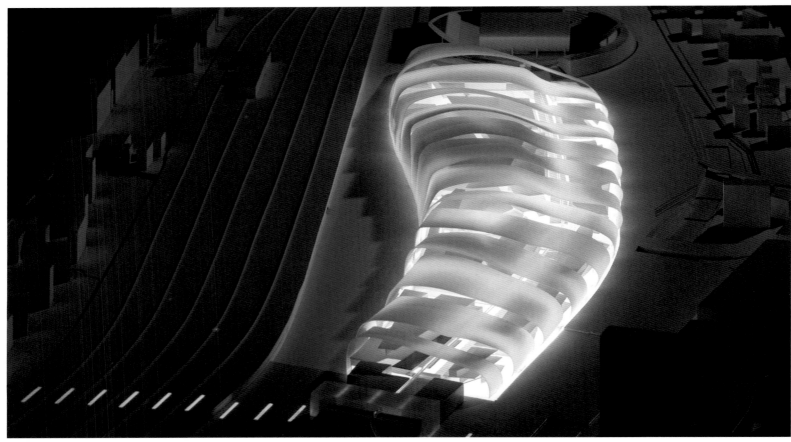

↑ | **Exterior**, roof   ↓ | **Sections**

Multi Casa Duisburg
Duisburg

In its union with the Königsstrasse, Multi Casa has created a new cultural and commercial stretch that, starting in the inner city, crosses the main station to meet Duisburg's new landmark, the MSV Stadium. The building is an emblem of economical and future-oriented architecture. Planar façades of glass as well as wing-like metal scales on the surface of the building let the onlooker experience the inner and outer aspects structure each time anew. The interior interconnected space was created in such a way, that the simple concrete ceilings offer the highest possible flexibility and use. Any part of the mall can be reached from the underground garage or the parking lot on the ground level, both of which are integrated into the entirety of the complex using light wells that offer views of the green landscape stretching out in front. Greenery at the heart of the mall, park design uniting the area and the green oases created on the main station plaza – Multi Casa creates a truly variegated, green experience.

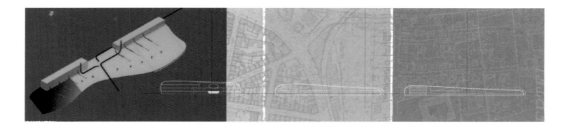

PROJECT FACTS

Address: area in the south of the main station, Duisburg, Germany. **Client** Philipp Holzmann BauProjekt AG (Multi Casa-Projektgemeinschaft). **Period of planning:** 1998–1999, not realized. **Gross floor area:** 375,000 m². **Estimated visitors:** approx. 26,000 per day. **Additional functions:** integration of Duisburg main station, casino, factory outlet, cinema, stadium, parking.

↑ | **Mall**
↓ | **Interior**

↑ | **Exterior,** planar façades of glass and wing-like metal scales
↓ | **Interior**

de Architekten Cie.

↑ | **Interior**
→ | **Mall**

De Klanderij

Enschede

The post-war building of the mall at the inner city border was resurrected according to a
new plan. The building's volume, originally hermetic, was transformed into a part of the
city space. Around the block, the construction is not identical on all sides, but changes in
height and surface texture to break up the mass of the volume. The revitalized city continues on the roof of the mall, where a garden landscape encircles apartment units accessed
by a ramp.

PROJECT FACTS

Address: H.J. van Heekplein 58-17, 7511 HN Enschede, The Netherlands. **CI ent:** ForumInvest B.V. Prowinko Groep B.V. **Period of construction:** 2002–2004. **Gross floor area:** 30,000 m². **Additional function:** residential. **Principle of urban development:** MVRDV. **Interior architect:** David Rogers, The Jerde Partnership.

↑ | **Interior**, detail
← | **Aerial**

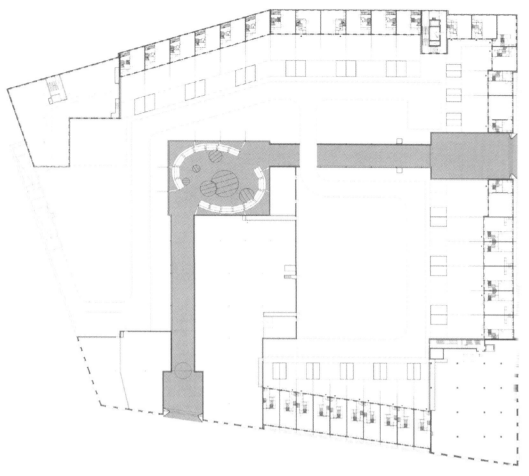

←| Floor plan
↙| Exterior

RKW Rhode Kellermann
Wawrowsky Architektur +
Städtebau

↑ | **Bar in the core of the center**
→ | **Atrium,** ground floor and basement

Sevens
Düsseldorf

At the core of the Sevens shopping center is a generous open space which extends over seven levels and opens up at the top. The silhouette of the glazed mall roof rises above the roofs of the city, letting the glass façade peak act as a landmark on the Königsallee. Horizontal shopping movements are redirected in vertical open spaces. The themes of retail and changing consumer behavior patterns demand high visibility and transparency. Natural light, reduced numbers of different material used and color provide an appropriate ambience.

PROJECT FACTS

Address: Königsallee 56, 40212 Düsseldorf, Germany. **Client:** Sevens Düsseldorf GbR. **Period of construction:** 1999–2000. **Gross floor area:** 35,700 m².

≒←| Atrium
← | Exterior
↓ | Mall

Josef Paul Kleihues,
Kleihues + Kleihues

↑ | **Dome**
→ | **Exterior**

Galeria Kaufhof Alexanderplatz
Berlin

The Galeria Kaufhof on Alexanderplatz has a history that is as colorful as its surroundings.
The store's origins lie with the Hermann Tietz Department Store, which was built on this
area at the beginning of the 20th Century. The Centrum Emporium occupied the space as
a fine example of 1970's zeitgeist. The current reconstruction and expansion of the Kaufhof building took place between 2004 and 2006. The building's character is defined by its
new façade, which is a modern interpretation of classic department store architecture that
includes large entrances, a two-story plinth and sculpturally structured natural stone surfaces. The domed, light-filled atrium with escalators is at the center of the building.

PROJECT FACTS

Address: Alexanderplatz 9, 10178 Berlin, Germany. **Client:** Kaufhaus Warenhaus am Alex GmbH. **Period of construction:** 2004–2006. **Gross floor area:** 75,000 m². **Architect original building:** Josef Kaiser and Günter Kunert, 1967–1970.

↑ | **Exterior,** Dirksenstraße next to the station
Alexanderplatz
← | **Section**
↙ | **Ground floor plan**
→ | **Escalators**

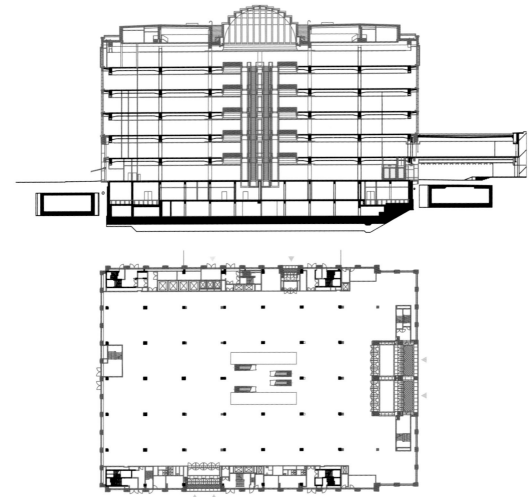

Chapman Taylor Architetti
Milano

↑ | **Escalator**
→ | **Stairway**

Il Giulia

Trieste

With the restyling of an historic commercial center in 2004–2006, il Giulia was the first shopping center in town. The property, which is conveniently located in a central densely populated neighborhood, has 50 units and a GLA of approx. 15,200 m² over three levels. The aim was to completely renew the external and internal spaces without changing functionality. Chapman Taylor Architects used new shapes and materials in order to create an innovative architectural approach.

PROJECT FACTS

Address: Via Giulia 75/3, Trieste, Italy. **Client:** Schroder Property Investment Management (Italy). **Period of construction:** 2004–2006. **Gross floor area:** 14,856 m². **Estimated visitors:** approx. 10,000 per day. **Additional functions:** children area. **Project team:** Gerardo Sannella (leader), Gianluca Follo, Kristina Madirazza (architects). **Construction drawings:** Spav (exterior), Coiver (interior). **Lighting design:** Artemide.

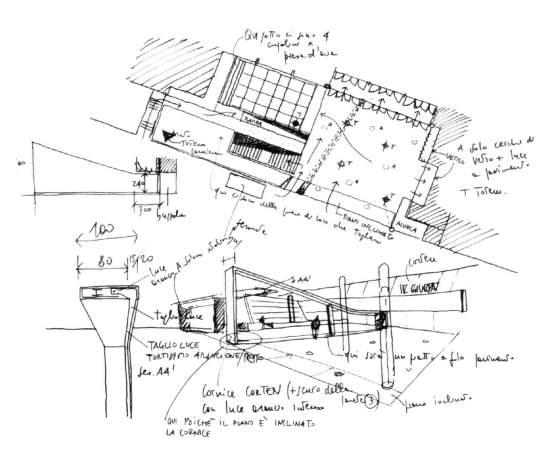

←← | Top view of the stairway
↙ | Outdoor entrance square at night
← | First sketches of the external square
↓ | Escalator top view

José Guedes Cruz

Ponte de Lima Municipal Market

Ponte de Lima

The restoration of the market built in 1927 had to include remodeling of the existing shops, addition of new retail spaces and building an underground garage. The east and south wings had to be demolished and were replaced by a new wing with two levels of shops. This turned a rectangular complex into a U-shaped market, and gave it an interior open to the city and the river. The base that is now used for parking and the three previously existing wings are clearly distinct from the new roof and the new wing of shops. The original structures, in traditional robust masonry, maintain their commitment to the site and guard against the violence of the river's flood waters. The new elements, made of wood and covered in copper and glass, breathe lightness and transparency, filling the square with light and shadow and bringing the traditional market to life.

PROJECT FACTS

Address: R. do Mercado, 4990 Ponte de Lima, Portugal. **Client:** City Hall of Ponte de Lima. **Period of construction:** 1998–2002. **Gross floor area:** 4,998 m². **Estimated visitors:** approx. 1,400 per day. **Structural engineering:** Proença e Neves.

↑ | **Entrance**
← | **Façade**

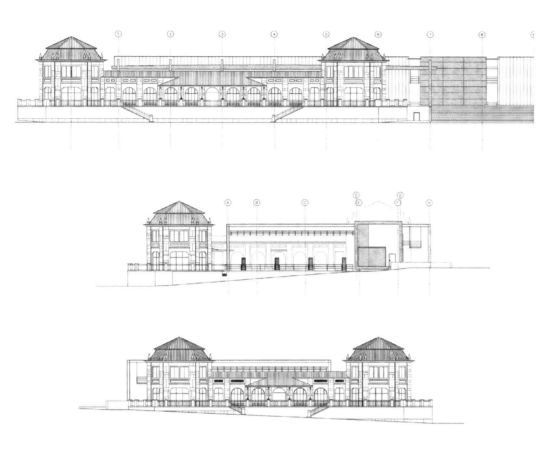

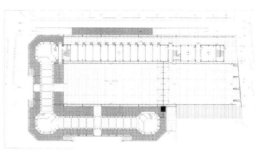

← | Sections
↙ | Detail stairs
↑ | Floor plan
↓ | Exterior

↑ | **View to light tunnel**
→ | **Atrium**

PALLADIUM

Prague

A unique shopping and services center was created in the heart of historical Prague with
the opening of the Palladium. In addition to retail and gastronomic spaces as well as
places for artistic events, the complex offers flexible-use office space and a three-story
below-ground garage with a 900-car capacity. Two highly prized, historic buildings (an
old barracks and a riding hall from 1859) have been integrated into the concept. Interconnected and accessible via two entrances are over 160 stores and more than 30 restaurants
on five levels. The latter are found on the topmost floor, and form a unique constellation
of Central European epicurean offerings.

PROJECT FACTS

Address: Namesti Republiky, Praha 1, Czech Republic. **Client:** EURO-PROPERTY-FUND s.r.o. **Period of construction:** 2005–2007. **Gross floor area:** 115,000 m². **Estimated visitors:** approx. 50,000 per day. **Additional functions:** offices. **Structural engineering:** Vasko + Partner Ingenieure. **Interior design:** RTKL. **Lighting design:** Bliss-Fasman. **Building services:** HTW.

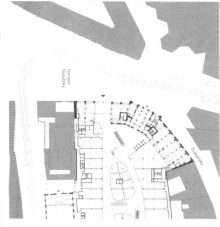

←← | **Atrium**
← | **Exterior**
⌒ | **Site plan**
〜 | **Exterior**, from street Na Porici

Hans Ruijssenaars
Architecten

↑ | **Exterior**
↗ | **Interior**
→ | **Sketch**
→→| **Sections,** original (top) and new parts
(below)

Magna Plaza
Amsterdam

The former main postal office has been restored, however the only façade feature that received significant alterations was the main entrance due to its high frequency of use. The original plan foresaw public use of just the ground level of the building. The restructuring makes use of the existing galleries around a light well, continuing them around two additional light wells and into the opened-up basement. Escalators were inserted into the spaces, and rooms were expanded by removing all non-load bearing walls. The new steel frame and concrete elements pick up the color scheme of the original parts.

PROJECT FACTS

Address: Nieuwezijds Voorburgwal, Amsterdam, The Netherlands. **Client:** Magna Plaza bv. **Period of construction:** 1988–1993. **Gross floor area:** 8,500 m². **Estimated visitors:** 6000 per day. **Architect original building:** H. Peters (1874–1932).

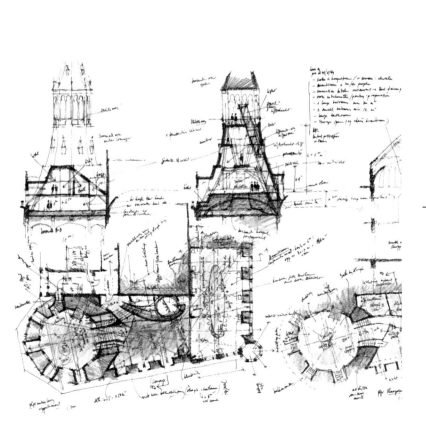

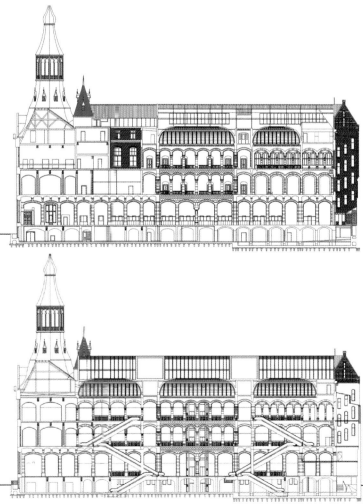

↑ | **Frame in brick**
→ | **Front façade**

Twentec

Enschede

The Twentec shopping center is part of a large scale urban renewal project called Van Heekplein in the center of the Dutch town Enschede. To attract customers, a strong architectural gesture is introduced: a brick tower, followed by a 120 meter long, four meter high glazed structure, ending in the name of the project as a four meter high brick element. A diverse and thematic lighting plan for the glazed structure enhances the urban quality of the van Heekplein and also strengthens the exposure of the shopping center as a whole. The detailing of the glazed structure as well as the brick façade is very elaborate, giving this strong building a refined quality.

PROJECT FACTS
Address: Van Heekplein, Enschede, The Netherlands. **Client:** Foruminvest Naarden, The Netherlands. **Period of construction:** 2002–2004. **Gross floor area:** 9,000 m². **Estimated visitors:** approx. 10,000 per day. **Additional functions:** offices. **Urban plan Van Heekplein:** West 8, Henk Hartzema. **Light plan:** Cirque du Soleil.

↑ | **Rear façade**
← | **Shop entrance**

← | Tower
↙ | Ground floor plan
↓ | Front façade parking

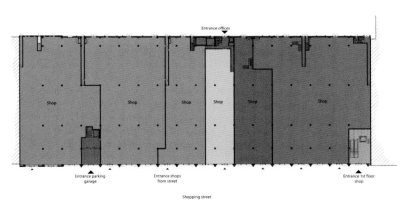

Shopping street

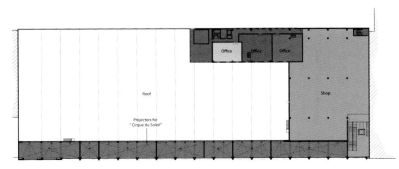

Dougall Design Associates, Inc., interior designers

↑ | Rotunda
→ | "Baroque" fountain

Forum Shops at Caesars Palace

Las Vegas

The Forum Shops are part of Caesar's Palace Hotel Casino. They have held on to their position as the most successful shopping malls in the USA through continual change and expansion. The latest addition is a large rotunda and a third level. Under clouds painted on the building's vaults one walks the streets of ancient Rome, but the citations do not limit themselves to antiquity, continuing on to Renaissance, Baroque and the 19th Century. The magnificent forms from various epoques are harmonized into a luxurious ensemble.

Address: 3500 S. Las Vegas Blvd., Las Vegas, NV 89109, USA. **Client:** Simon Property Group. **Completion:** 2004. **Gross floor area:** 65,775 m². **Estimated visitors:** approx. 50,000 per day. **Co-designer:** Marnell Corrao Associates. **Architects:** KGA Architecture.

↑ | **Exterior**
← | **Interior**

← | **Interior**, detail
↙ | **"Baroque" atrium**
↓ | **Entrance**

au4g / Valérie Justôme

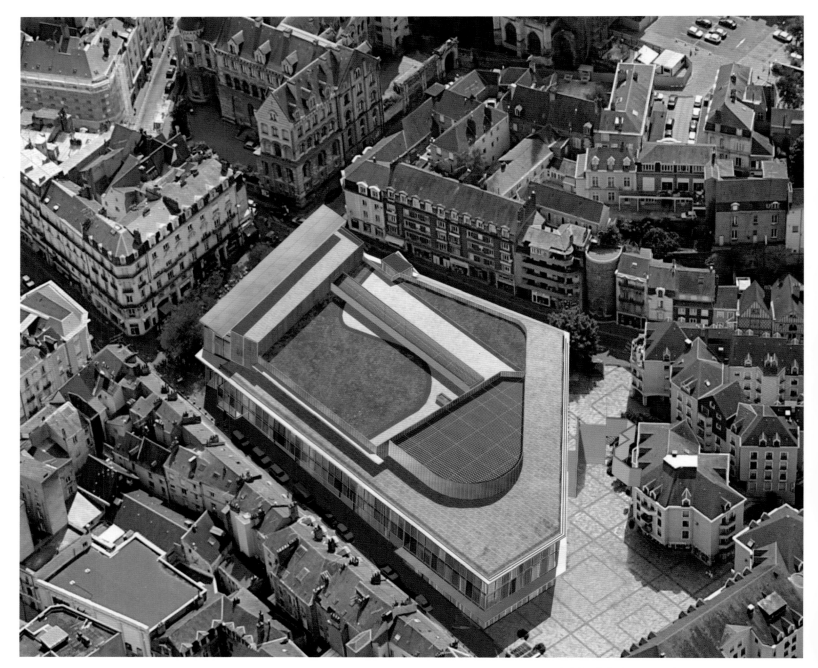

↑ | **Aerial photography**
↗ | **Exterior view by day,** Place Mondain-
Chanlouineau / Rue Plantagenêt
→ | **Exterior view by night,** Place Mondain-
Chanlouineau / Rue Plantagenêt

Fleur d'Eau
Angers

The location of the Fleur d'Eau, which opened in 2005, was earlier occupied by the "Les Halles", a shopping center from the 1970s. As the center lost its appeal, it was decided that a new building was needed to revive the area. The design of the new shopping center is based on the idea of openness. The façade consists up to 90% of glass, and depending on lighting conditions, its windows either reflect the surroundings or open up its interior to views. In addition, each side of the building is adjusted to height of the surrounding rows of homes, which lets the shopping center harmoniously integrate into the neighborhood.

PROJECT FACTS

Address: Place Mondain-Chanlouineau, Rue Plantagenêt, Place de la République, Rue Baudrière, 49000 Angers, France. **Client:** apsys. **Period of construction:** 2004–2005. **Gross floor area:** 13,350 m². **Structural engineering:** Even Structures. **Lighting design:** Bideau S.A.

PLAN RDC HAUT NIVEAU 31,50 MOYEN

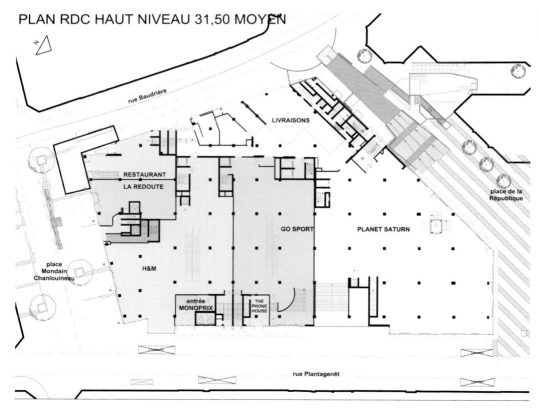

↑ | **Perspective,** view from Rue Baudrière
← | **Ground floor plan**

← | **Exterior view,** Place de la République to Tour Villebon

⌣ | **Perspective,** view from Place de la République

Sergei Tchoban
nps tchoban voss GbR Architekten BDA, A. M. Prasch
P. Sigl S. Tchoban E. Voss

↑ | **Exterior,** façade main entrance
→ | **Façade,** detail

New Department Store in the Europa Center

Berlin

The Europa Center, built in 1963–65 on Breitscheid square in Berlin Charlottenburg-Wilmersdorf, consists of thee structural components: a flat building housing the shopping center, hotel and cinema, the 85-meter-high office tower, and the garage on Nürnberger street. The Saturn media department store has been created within the existing ensemble, mostly within the section of the Kino Royal Palace. The building is horizontally structured into story-high layers which unite into a closed, planar façade and fan out or scale back into the tower. The glazing has a screen print with symbols from the world.

PROJECT FACTS

Address: Tauentzienstraße 9, 10789 Berlin, Germany. **Client:** 3 B Berliner Bau-Betreuung GmbH. **Period of construction:** 2006–2007. **Gross floor area:** 14,200 m². **Estimated visitors** approx. 11,000 per day. **Structural engineering:** LAP. **Architect original building:** Helmut Hentrich and Hubert Petschnigg (1963–65).

↑ | **The Europa Center**
← | **Window decoration,** 3rd floor

← | Façade, detail
↙ | Side entrance
↑↓ | Outline for window decoration

↑ | **Main entrance**
→ | **Interior glass balustrades**

Queens Plaza
Brisbane

The Queens Plaza is a compact retail gallery that links to an existing, four-block retail mall and a David Jones department store. The project's many challenges included the limited site size and the need to integrate with the two existing structures; the client's desire to attract premiere retail tenants; and the city-mandated requirement that the new retail center preserve the area's trademark architectural character. The resulting scheme blends contemporary design with the Edwardian, Victorian, and Gothic styles that define Brisbane's urban fabric. Australian sandstone and black granite clad the building's lower stories, calling to mind the rusticated bases of classical buildings, and metal detailing along the upper levels fosters a contemporary aesthetic.

PROJECT FACTS

Address: 226 Queen Street, Brisbane City QLD 4000, Australia. **Client:** Colonial First State Management (formerly Gandel Retail Management). **Period of construction:** 2003–2006. **Gross floor area:** 39,153 m². **Estimated visitors:** approx. 50,000 per day.

←← | **Design details,** give depth to building façade and provide shading
← | **Interior retail corridor**
↓ | **Façade,** with window display boxes

RKW Rhode Kellermann
Wawrowsky Architektur +
Städtebau

↑ | **Façade**
↗ | **Glass ceiling,** back area
→ | **Glass ceiling,** next to the main entrance

Stadtpalais Potsdam

Potsdam

After a 1995 fire in a roof truss, the largely unchanged 1920's department store located in the middle of a world heritage site of Potsdam's Baroque city quarter had to be refurbished. The listed façade of the steel frame structure on Bradenburger Straße was redeveloped along with the atrium with a painted glass roof. The original natural light illumination had to be replaced with artificial indirect light due to the addition of a floor. The glass panels were manually reconstructed using special glass and decorated after researching historical drawings, photos and color remainders. The new parts of the building carefully adjoin the original historical structure, nonetheless fulfilling modern demands of commercial architecture such as biophysical standards.

PROJECT FACTS

Address: Brandenburgerstr./ Jägerstr., 14467 Potsdam, Germany. **Client:** Karstadt Immobilien AG & Co. KG. **Period of construction:** 2003–2005. **Gross floor area:** 23,500 m². **Original building:** 1905–1907, Carl Schmanns (1913–14).

← – | **Atrium**
← | **Exterior,** heritage buildings
↓ | **Exterior,** main façade

SMC Alsop Architects

↑ | Leather Hotel

Walsall Waterfront

Walsall

Walsall waterfront, a seven-hectar area surrounding the New Art Gallery Walsall, is to be redeveloped by architect Will Alsop into a large shopping area on a strategic framework, and will include space for restaurants, cafés and a new hotel. It is part of a redevelopment rising on 17 acres of derelict land near Town Wharf and the canal arm featuring designer homes, "green" offices and public art. The goal is to produce an exciting mixed use, leisure-focused destination that takes advantage of the physical attributes of the site, extends the town center and encourages a mixture of architectural variety within the confines of an overall strategy, metaphorically and physically bridging lifestyle, urban greening and microclimatic enclosures for sustainability experiments. The canal is seen as an extension of the main street, with its turning point demarcated by an extraordinary object – the Leather Hotel. It is planned that this building will be clad in leather or a leather substitute as a reference to Walsalls' industrial history.

PROJECT FACTS

Address: Waterfront site, Walsall, UK. **Client:** Urban Splash. **Completion:** 2008. **Gross floor area:** 1,4741 m². **Additional functions:** residential, offices. **Masterplan:** SMC Alsop Architects. **Further buildings on the masterplan:** Shed KM, Querkraft.

↑ | **Section,** Leather Hotel and shopping center
↙ | **Sketch**

↓ | **Situation,** Waterfront shopping center and Leather Hotel

↖ | Travelator
↑ | Lift and escalator
↗ | Spiral staircase
→ | Hand drawings exterior
→→| Corner rue Gallieni / rue A. France

Espace Coty

Le Havre

In the city planning area of Coty, the historical image of the city of Le Havre meets against the areas of post-1945 reconstruction by Auguste Perret. In 1999 saw the opening of Espace Coty with its countless pedestrian and entry zones. The interior is designed fittingly for the harbor city to the theme of the sea. Stairs and railings recall their nautical counterparts, on the second floor "the command bridge" swings above the mall, and some walls are painted to resemble the exterior of passenger ships. Brick and concrete dominate the exterior.

Address: 22, rue Casimir Périer, 76 600 Le Havre, France. **Client:** ALTAFEA / MAB. **Completion:** 1999. **Gross floor area:** 27,000 m². **Co-architects:** Agence Tribel, Agence Brocard, Agence Bernet. **Structural engineering:** Cabinet Mizrahi. **Landscape design:** Atelier Grunig-Tribel.

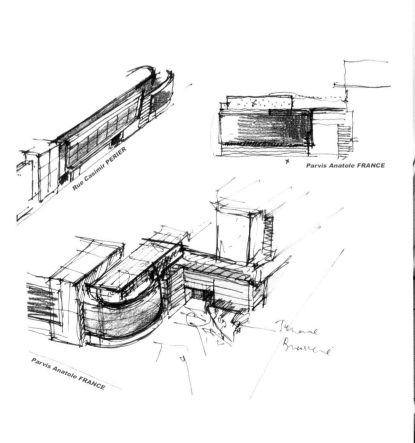

Rue Casimir PERIER

Parvis Anatole FRANCE

Parvis Anatole FRANCE

↑ | **Q207,** view through one of the 12 glass cones
into Galerie Lafayette
↗ | **Q207,** glass cone
→ | **Q207,** façade

Friedrichstadtpassagen
Berlin

The buildings along Friedrichstraße are connected to each other via underground walkways, and occupy the 205th, 206th and 207th blocks, or quarters, on the city's master
plan. The Q205, the only complete block structure, appropriates the Berlin block, with
the cuboid structures typical for its form, as its theme. Quartier Q206 contrasts this ex-
tremely regular architectural concept with its neo-expressive angular elements like the
"star" dome, the dissolved façade as well as interior design that evokes the art deco style.
The Q207 with its main occupant, Galeries Lafayette, sets itself apart from the block and
the cast stone perforated façade with a completely glazed, modern curved exterior. The
interior is punctuated with variations on glass cones that evoke the domes of the famous
Parisian flagship store.

PROJECT FACTS

Address: Friedrichsstraße 67–78, 10117 Berlin, Germany. **Client:** Tishman Speyer Proper (Q205), Fundus Gruppe Jagdfeld (Q206), Euro-Projektentwicklung (Q207). **Period of construction:** 1993–1995 (Q205), 1992–1995 (Q206, Q207). **Gross floor area:** 48,748 m² (Q205), 23,300 m² (Q206), 31,600 m² (Q207). **Additional functions:** offices, residential.

↑ | **Q205**, façade
← | **Q205**, entrance

← | **Q205**, exterior detail
↙ | **Q205**, atrium with sculpture "Tower of Clythe"
by John Chamberlain
↓ | **Q205**, interior detail

↑ | **Q206**, view onto the skylight
← | **Q206**, atrium

← | **Q206**, detail in art deco style
↙ | **Q206**, façade
↓ | **Q206**, interior detail

↑ | **Shade-giving and cooling structures,** detail
→ | **Street, roofed over with ETFE foil cushions**

Clarke Quay quarter

Singapore

The diamond-shaped site houses a series of traditional shop houses with well-proportioned colonnades along its waterfront by the Singapore River. To revive the riverfront, the architects created a series of raised "lily pad" platforms and "bluebell" membrane canopies to animate the water's edge. Installation of shade-giving and cooling structures spread throughout the streets mitigates the extremeness of the Singapore's environment. The streets are roofed over with ETFE foil cushions supported on steelwork structures. These structures are known as "environmental angels", and act as chimney vents, providing shade and encouraging ventilation at ground level through both passive and active means.

PROJECT FACTS

Address: Clarke St, Singapore. **Client:** Capitaland. **Period of construction:** 2002–2003. **Gross floor area:** 18,500 m². **Estimated visitors:** approx. 3,000 per day. **Additional functions:** offices, market, club.

← ← | Along the riverside
↙ ↙ | "Lily pad" platforms
← | ETFE foil cushions
↙ | Steelwork structures
↑ | Situation
↓ | Site plan

de Architekten Cie.

↑ | **"UFO"**, view from the promenades
→ | **"UFO" and residential units**

Spazio

Zoetermeer

The expansion of the center to the west of Zoetermeer was necessitated by the strong growth of the new city. Spazio should revive the intersection point of both centers with a mixture of shopping, leisure, residential and office space. A promenade with two bordering shopping floors cuts through the building volume. Resting on both sections above the promenade, a prominent "UFO" is found. This emblematic volume houses a fitness center. The towers with residential units and a row of offices stand above the shopping floors.

PROJECT FACTS
Address: Westwaarts, Centrum West, 2711 Zoetermeer, The Netherlands. **Client:** Amvest Amsterdam. **Period of construction:** 2001–2006. **Gross floor area:** 80,000 m². **Additional functions:** residential, offices, public transport, fitness center. **Co-architects:** Fritz van Dongen, Branimir Medić & Pero Puljiz. **Structural engineering:** Smit Westerman. **Urban plan:** OMA.

←← | Exterior
← | Promenade

↑ | **Glass sculpture**
→ | **Interior view**

The Oracle
Reading

The design concept had to introduce a regional-scale shopping center into an existing town. The integration of the development was achieved by means of architecture and by establishing a new loop promenade. The scheme's overall mass was divided into visually separate buildings through three-dimensional interplay of form used on the elevations that are sensitive to Reading's architectural traditions. One of the key breakthroughs in the design of the concept was the recognition of the River Kennet as an asset to be used as the focus of the new public space, rather than an obstacle which split the site in half. The Oracle's retail tenants were encouraged to express their brands' identities through their shop fronts.

PROJECT FACTS

Address: Bridge Street, Reading, Berkshire RG1 2AG, United Kingdom. **Cl ent:** Hammerson. **Period of construction:** 1997–1999. **Gross floor area:** 72,279 m². **Estimated visitors:** approx. 52,000 per day. **Additional functions:** childrens play area, cinema, community facilities right club.

←← | **Night view of cinema and performance area**

↙↙ | **Main entrance to The Oracle,** from the riverside

↙ | **Riverside,** showing canopy

← | **The Oracle at night**

↓ | **Aerial**

Klein Dytham architecture
(KDa)

↑ | Interior
→ | Shop façade

Selfridges Co. Wonder Room
London

Selfridges is fast approaching its 100th year. Back when Henry Gordon Selfridge founded the first store on Oxford Street, his vision was to bring wonders from across the globe to amaze and excite his customers. The Wonder Room project was a chance to reintroduce those elements of surprise and wonder to the ground floor of this store and create a department store with Kunstkammer and Curiosity Cabinet qualities for the 21st Century. The key element of the design is an elegant screen of fins running around the perimeter of the room, with strict display cases placed between them. Along Orchard Street, windows have been opened up allowing views through the new Wonder Bar and Concept Store area.

PROJECT FACTS **Address:** 400 Oxford Street, London W1A 1AB, United Kingdom. **Client:** Selfridges. **Period of construction:** 2007. **Gross floor area:** 1,900 m².

↑ | Shop
← | Interior

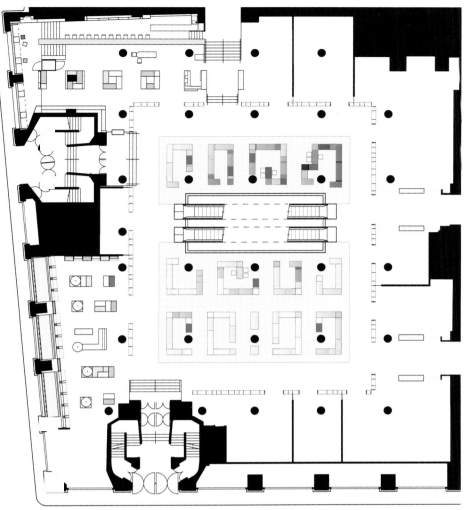

Floor plan, Wonder Room

Shop, façade detail

RTKL Associates Inc.

↑ | **View of Bloomingdale's from Mission
Street**
→ | **The restored central rotunda**

Westfield San Francisco Centre
San Francisco

The Emporium department store on Market Street was once hailed as the "grandest mercantile building in the world," and its design elements that include a Beaux-Arts grand façade and a signature glass dome were among the most recognizable in the city. In recent decades, the Emporium building stood vacant and fell into disrepair. After an eight-year development and design process, the site, now home to Westfield San Francisco Centre, showcases the Emporium's historic elements and integrates an existing retail center located on an adjacent site. The 500,000 lb dome was raised 58 feet and suspended on a newly built foundation while the rest of the building was constructed around it. The façade restoration engages the surrounding cityscape and has added new energy to the district.

PROJECT FACTS

Address: 835 Market Street, San Francisco, California, USA. **Client:** Westfeld Emporium LLC / Forest City Development. **Period of construction:** 2004–2006. **Gross floor area:** 1 9,500 m². **Additional functions:** offices, academic space, transit station. **Assistant design architect** John Pederson Fox Associates. **Structural engineering:** Nabih Youssef & Associates. **Lighting designer:** Horton Lees Brogden Lighting Design. **Acoustical engineer:** Thorburn & Associates. **Architect original building:** Carey & Company (1895).

↑ | Dome details
← | Entrance
↗ | Interior corridors
→ | Skylights provide natural lighting
→→ | Views to dining venues and retail
levels

↑ | **Interior foodcourt**
→ | **Aerial**

ZŁOTE TARASY

Warsaw

Surrounding the interior plaza, a three-level retail and entertainment center is organized in terraces, as suggested by the project's name which means "golden terraces". Towers rising above the three-level center will house office space. Designed to weave the urban fabric of central Warsaw back together, the center recreates the historic urban grid that was lost during World War II and revitalize public spaces nearby. Located near the Warszawa Centralna train station and the Palace of Culture, the mall is a landmark destination and the center of a large urban system of the city's proposed new high-rise district. Designed as an extension of the city's "necklace" of historic parks, the plaza is enclosed by an innovative glass roof with an undulating surface inspired by tree canopies.

PROJECT FACTS

Address: Ul. Złota 59, 00-120 Warszawa, Poland. **Client:** ING Real Estate. **Completion:** 2007. **Gross floor area:** 185,800 m². **Estimated visitors:** approx. 60,000 per day. **Additional functions:** office, multiplex cinema, entertainment. **Structural engineering:** Arup. **Landscape design:** EDAW. **Lighting consultant:** Kaplan, Gehring, McCarroll Architectural Lighting.

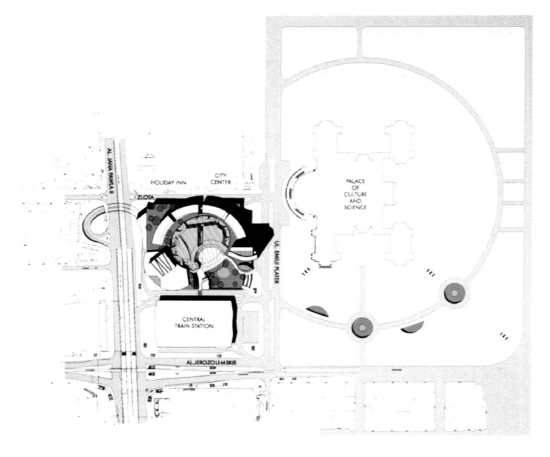

←←| **Interior,** circulation path to connect the train station with the historic city center
← | **Masterplan area,** for the Palace of Culture
↓ | **Exterior,** physical and visual connector to the adjacent Warszawa Centralna

Josef Paul Kleihues
and Norbert Hensel,
Kleihues + Kleihues

↑ | **Courtyard Picassohof**
→ | **Façade**

Münster Arkaden

Münster

The customer hall with 41 stores is at the heart of the Münster Arkaden. The arms of the passage fold around each other at the center to form a square covered by a glass dome. The architectonic concept consciously does not hold itself to conventional standards, but picks up on the concepts of historical galleries and tries to reinterpret these. Constantly new visual relationships and a canon of architectural focal points create an exciting space. The façade with individual natural stone cladding is structured klin a way that creates an impression of single houses. This technique refers to the delicacy and detail of the city center, with the old Münster architecture picked up in the color play of the main market.

PROJECT FACTS
Address: Ludgeristraße 100, 48143 Münster, Germany. **Client:** Sparkassen-Grundstücksverwaltungs GmbH & Co. KG. **Period of construction:** 2002–2006. **Gross floor area:** 53.056 m². **Additional functions:** offices, parking.

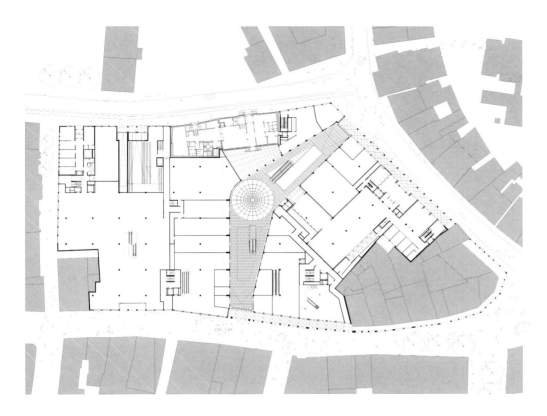

←← | Rotunda
↙ | Passage
← | Ground floor plan
↓ | Passage

RTKL Associates Inc. and
Design 103 International

↑ | Views of escalator paths
→ | Main entrance atrium

Siam Paragon

Bangkok

"The Pride of Bangkok" is Thailand's first mega shopping complex. It houses many of the world's most prestigious high-end brands and has made an immediate impact on the area by transforming the surrounding district into a region of bustling activity. The biggest challenge for the design team was the creation of a circulation plan and layout. Strategic retail groupings and floor arrangements help minimize pedestrian congestion, supporting a traffic plan that moves shoppers conveniently throughout the center's spaces. Siam Paragon has truly become one of Bangkok's most celebrated destinations, drawing tourists from around the world to its cultural, retail and entertainment selections.

PROJECT FACTS

Address: 991/1 Rama 1 Road, Pathumwan Bangkok 10330, Thailand. **Client:** Siam Paragon Development Company Limited. **Period of construction:** 2003–2006. **Gross floor area:** 7,764 m². **Estimated visitors:** approx. 250,000 per day. **Additional functions:** cultural center, supermarket, bowling alley, 21-screen cinema, IMAX theater. **Graphic designer:** Mende Kaoru. **Lighting designer:** Bensley Design Studio. **Landscape architect:** Thai Obayashi Corp., Ltd.

← Upscale food court seating
↙ Multiple level escalator circulation
← Main entrance, exterior
↙ Floor plan
↓ Interior retail activity

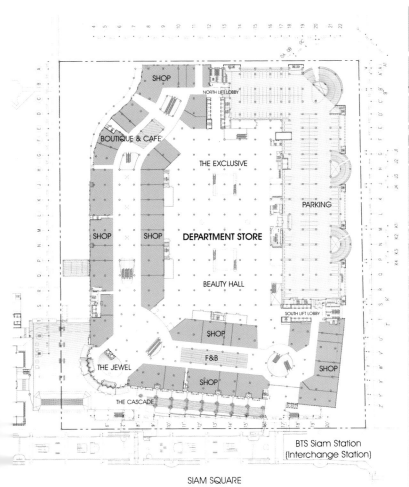

SHOP

NORTH LIFT LOBBY

BOUTIQUE & CAFE'

THE EXCLUSIVE

PARKING

SHOP   SHOP   DEPARTMENT STORE

BEAUTY HALL

SOUTH LIFT LOBBY

SHOP

F&B   SHOP

THE JEWEL

SHOP

THE CASCADE

BTS Siam Station
(Interchange Station)

SIAM SQUARE

Klein Dytham architecture
(KDa)

↑ | **Interior**, façade
→ | **Façade by night**

R3 ukishima / aicafe54

Naha

The four-unit commercial building is located just off Kokusai Dori, the location of many trendy boutiques and galleries, and where Okinawa's tradition and young culture meet. The site had a long street frontage facing the side of a bland convenience store, and onto which all four retail units, including the café, had to face. A 25-meter long, five meter-high perforated concrete block screen, ubiquitous to Okinawa, was erected, enclosing a balcony access to the second floor while screening off the convenience store and electrical and telephone wires running along the street. The screen with its pixilated pink orchid pattern creates an encapsulated world for the cafe while letting the air and light into the building.

PROJECT FACTS

Address: 2-1-13 Matsuo, Nahashi, Okinawa, Japan. **Client:** Risa Partners Inc. **Period of construction:** 2006–2007. **Gross floor area:** 492 m². **Structural engineering:** Arup Japan

↑ | **Façade**, by day
← | **First floor plan**

← | **Exterior**, by night
↓ | **Interior**, aicafe54

↑ | **Atrium**, including faceted granite walls
→ | **Exterior**, fissured stone façade and nine-level glass atrium

Langham Place
Hong Kong

In the heart of Mongkok, a city known for its diverse markets and frenetic street life, a four-block site was redeveloped with a mixed-use project that would serve as an economic catalyst to revitalize the entire district. Langham Place builds on and evolves Mongkok's appeal by supplementing the low-to-mid retail market with high-quality tenants and adding the area's first five-star hotel and class A office tower. The design blends into and vertically extends Mongkok's vibrant street experience. A nine-story glass atrium reveals activity within to passersby. Innovative circulation techniques, such as multi-level express escalators and a spiraling retail-lined path, move people effortlessly between the 15-level center's 300 shops and restaurants. A continuous multi-media show projected onto the ceiling of the atrium invites people inside the center and on the streets below to enjoy the dining and entertainment hub on the top levels.

PROJECT FACTS
Address: 8 Argyle Street, Mongkok, Kowloon, Hong Kong. **Client:** Great Eagle Holdings Ltd. **Completion:** 2005. **Gross floor area:** 168,222 m². **Estimated visitors:** approx. 100,000 per day. **Additional functions:** office, hotel, residential, government, entertainment, cinema.

←← | Four-level "expresscalators"
← | View to the Digital Sky from the atrium
↙ | Stone façade of the retail center
↓ | Interior, communal space featuring restaurants and entertainment

↑ | **Exterior**
↗ | **Façade**, window detail
↗↗ | **Section**, façade
→ | **Floor plan**
→→| **Exterior**

Shopping Center De Vlinder, Vroom & Dreesman

Emmen

The existing department store built in the 1960's was dated and did not meet the requirements and desires of the contemporary shopper. Its old, concrete paneled façades have been replaced by a lighter, glazed cladding. The curved glazed façade combines the various shops in one material gesture and produces different effects: reflective, transparent, translucent. The department store has also been reorganized internally with the addition of a gallery, apartments on six stories and smaller shop outlets. A new public passage on the ground floor changes the arrangement of the shopping center, giving it a stronger directional structure.

PROJECT FACTS
Address: Mondriaanplein 10, Emmen, The Netherlands. **Client:** Multi Vastgoed. **Period of construction:** 1994–1996. **Gross floor area:** 10,294 m².

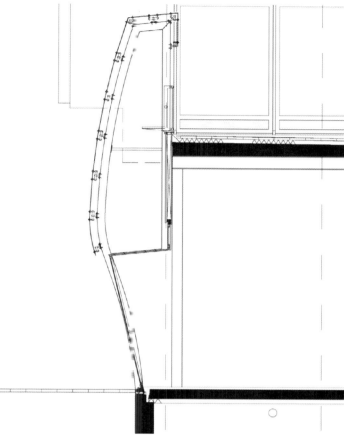

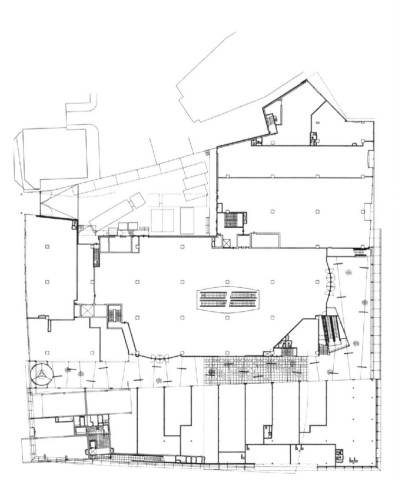

↑ | **Plaza**
↗ | **Village-environment**
→ | **Cathedral building,** with a modern glass tower

La Cittadella
Kawasaki

La Cittadella is the new heart of Kawasaki and the first step toward rejuvenating the surrounding area. The site of the city's famous and newly relocated Club Citta, La Cittadella combines dining, shopping, cinema and nightclubs into a new place that will define the urban experience for residents and visitors. It features a gently sloping hill climb circulation that carries visitors effortlessly from the street level, past cafes, shops and restaurants to the upper-level entertainment district. The cascading design is layered with landscaped terraces, bridges and stepped gardens with rich colors and textures. Organized into three districts that create round-the-clock activity, future phases of the project include additional retail and plans for a 14-level residential tower.

PROJECT FACTS

Address: La Cittadella, 4-1 Ogawamachi, Kawasaki, Japan. **Client:** Misu Entertainment, Inc. **Completion:** 2003. **Gross floor area:** 58,578 m². **Estimated visitors:** approx. 12,500 per day. **Additional functions:** cinema, nightclubs, residential.

↑ | **Plaza**
← | **Aerial,** showing the cascading effect

÷ | **Exterior stair**
↓ | **Elevations**

ELS Architecture and
Urban Design

↑ | **16th Street Mall,** day view, looking
northwest
→ | **Glenarm Place,** night view, looking south-
west

Denver Pavilions

Denver

Denver Pavilions was one of the first urban retail / entertainment centers to be built in
the United States. It helped revitalize the western end of the downtown, which lacked
activity after business hours. The open-air layout supports its role as a community center.
The project follows the concept of assembling the country's most sought-after retailers
and entertainment venues in an open-air environment that is part of the existing urban
fabric. In order to fit into the scale and fabric of the historic district, the Pavilions center
is composed of four distinct building elements linked by streets and bridges. The unifying
Great Wall, spelling out Denver, is an icon for the city.

PROJECT FACTS

Address: 500 16th Street, Suite 10, Denver, Colorado 80202, USA. **Client:** Entertainment Development Group. **Period of construction:** 1997–1998. **Gross floor area:** 37,000 m². **Estimated visitors:** approx. 28,770 per day. **Additional functions:** movie theatre, bowling alley. **Civil engineer:** Martin & Martin. **Structural engineering:** L.A. Fuess Partners Inc. **Construction management:** Wells Partnership, Inc. **Acoustic design:** Charles Salter Associates. **Light design:** George Sexton Associates. **General contractor:** Hensel Phelps Construction Company.

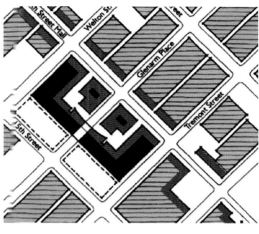

←←| **Great Wall and retail bridge over
Glenarm Place**
← | **16th Street Mall**, Arcade Entry
↑ | **Denver pavilion**, site diagram
↓ | **16th Street Mall**, looking southeast

↑ | **Exterior**
↗ | **Façade,** with an extensive exterior lighting
scheme and the so-called "lines of light"
↗↗ | **Atrium,** skylight
→ | **Façade,** view to the atrium, detail
→→| **Atrium**

Vershina Trade and Entertainment Center

Surgut

The Trade and Entertainment Center, the first five-star international shopping center in Surgut, comprises retail spaces, extreme sports areas, dance studios, restaurants, bars and an underground night club. The building will provide around-the-clock activities for all visitors, both young and old. The concept for the building is based on the dialectical play between dark and light, solid and transparent, open and closed. The result is an introverted building with several strategically positioned cuts (openings) through which visitors can view the surroundings. It is equipped with an extensive exterior lighting scheme, and its glass façade will form a screen onto which moving advertisements can be projected.

PROJECT FACTS

Address: Intersection of Mir Avenue and General Ivanov Street, Surgut, Russian Federation. **Client:** SKU. **Period of construction:** 2005–2008. **Gross floor area:** 36,200 m². **Additional functions:** indoor roller dome, skateboard rink, indoor climbing wall, parking.

↖↑ | Interior
← | Foyer

← | **Atrium**
↙ | **Floor plans,** mezzanine and third floor
↓ | **Interior**

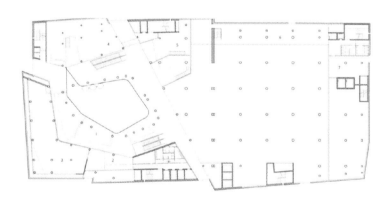

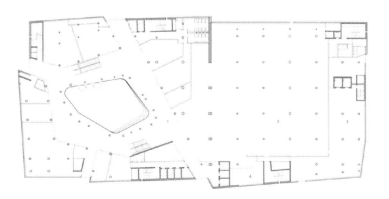

Jean Nouvel

↑ | **Exterior**
↗ | **Façade**
→ | **Interior**

Le Triangle des Gares

Lille

The new city quarter of Lille was created during the restructuring of the TGV express railroad to lay down the Eurostar Paris-London track. Stars of the architectural world were invited to build in the neighborhood. Le Triangle des Gares between the Lille Europe and Lille Flandres stations is a busy district that expresses this via Jean Nouvel's style: Graphic elements and interior detailing take the world of air travel and Formula 1 as their inspiration. On the exterior, signaling symbols, escalators, fly-overs and dynamically rounded building volumes create a corresponding impression. A group of 120 retail stores is centered around a supermarket.

PROJECT FACTS

Address: Le Corbusier, avenue Willy Brandt, 59000 Lille, France. **Client:** SCCTG (Capri & Espace Promotion). **Period of construction:** 1991–1994. **Gross floor area:** 155,000 m². **Additional functions:** housing, business school, offices, hotel, concert halls. **Masterplan:** Rem Koolhaas.

Louis Karol

↑ | **Exterior**

↓ | **Section**

Victoria Wharf Mall

Cape Town

The Victoria Wharf Mall is the biggest of the seven shopping centers located on the Victoria and Albert Waterfront, and is its main attraction. The rebuilding of the former harbor into a city center had significantly influenced Louis Karol. Before the Waterfront was erected, Cape Town was dead at night. After just a short time, the successful mall had to be expanded. Victorian industrial architecture, particularly of warehouses, determined the layout of the volumes and their contours. The execution of façade details, however, is varied in a modern way. A light-filled double-level center which integrates itself into the historical situation and simultaneously fulfils its modern function is the result.

Address: Quay 5 & Quay 6, V&A Waterfront, Waterfront, Cape Town, South Africa. **Client:** Victoria & Alfred Waterfront (Pty) Ltd. **Period of construction:** commenced 1991 (phase 1), completed 1996 (phase 2). **Gross floor area:** 89,000 m². **Estimated visitors:** approx. 65,000 per day. **Additional function:** cinema complex.

↑ | **Entrance**

↓ | **Section Mall**

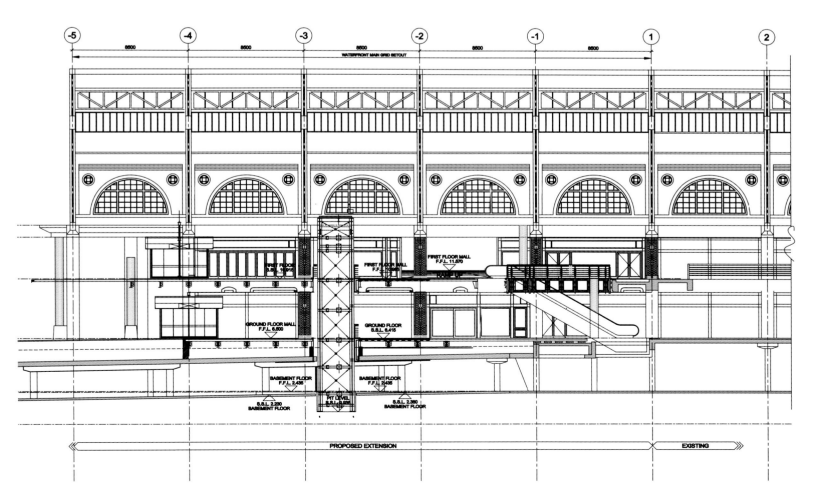

↑ | **Interior,** detail
↗ | **Resting area**
→ | **Shop window**

Magazin Kenzo
Paris

Following Kenzo's philosophy, each store recalls a specific garden, representing the brands in connection with nature, urbanity and exoticism. The interior design of the two Parisian stores refers to the gardens of Katasura in Kyoto. The flooring is of recomposed stone, reproducing the rough and irregular aspect of the alleys. The resting areas are subdued, intimate and bathe in diffused light punctuated by selected spot lighting. Matte white walls with adhesive flowers complete the overall perspective of an fall clearing in a volume of no visible limits.

Address: Boutique Hommes , 27 bd Madeleine 75008 Paris, France. **Client:** Kenzo. **Architects:** Vudafieri Partners / Simona Quadri.

↑ | Interior
← | Stairs to the upper floor

← | Stairs to the upper floor
↓ | Sections

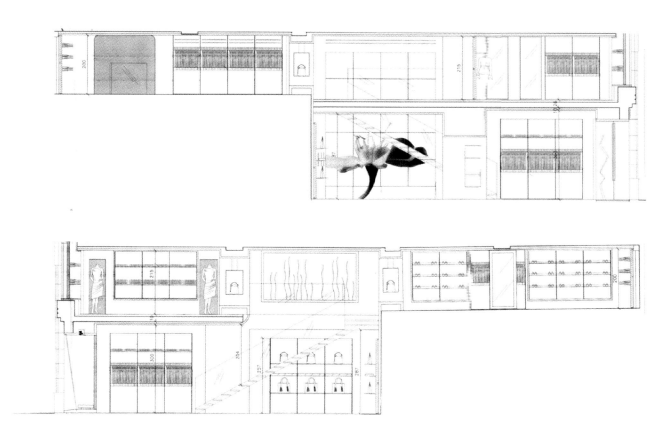

↑ | **Exterior**, façade
→ | **Interior**, façade

P&C department store
Cologne

Set on Cologne's central Schildergasse, the new Peek & Cloppenburg flagship store is a savant blend of glass, steel, stone and wood: classic materials to dress a modern building, entirely dedicated to fashion. The glass house, which is 130 meters long and up to 34 meters high, is reminiscent of a 19th Century orangery. Sixty-six timber girders are connected like ribs to the steel ridge girder, the three-dimensional, slightly curved, "backbone" of the body. Only every fourth to sixth of these wooden ribs rests directly on the skeleton. In between, the façade is a self-supporting construction, following the organic forms while safely absorbing the forces. Nestled into the curves, the glass rests lightly and encases the designer shops.

PROJECT FACTS
Address: Schildergasse 65–67, 50667 Cologne, Germany. **Client:** Peek & Cloppenburg. **Period of construction:** 1999–2005. **Gross floor area:** approx 23,000 m². **Consultants:** Knippers & Helbig, Büro Mosbacher, A.Walz. **General contractor:** Hochtief Construction.

←← | Exterior
← | Façade
↓ | View over Cologne

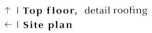
↑ | **Top floor,** detail roofing
← | **Site plan**

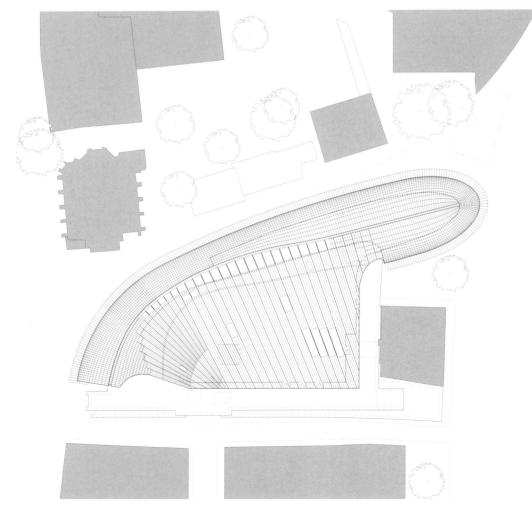

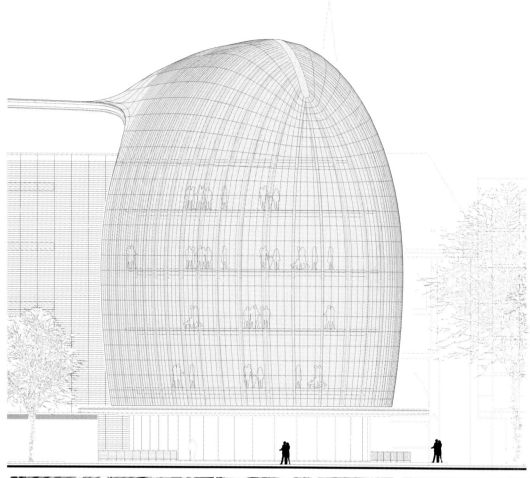

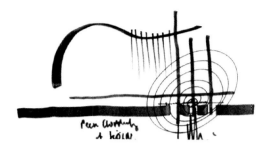

← | **Elevation**
↙ | **Interior**, detail
↑ | **Sketch**
↓ | **Interior**, detail

↑ | **Atrium**
→ | **Main entrance**

City 2
Brussels

The renovation and enlargement of the largest shopping center in central Brussels took into account the spirit of the Bon Marché façade, a neighboring former department store, which is presently being rebuilt as an office building. The City 2 building was made higher by one setback floor to house an additional department store located under a new enlarged glass roof. This brought it closer to the size of neighboring buildings. The façade was re-clad with large display windows in powder-coated aluminum, while the rounded-off right angle of the main entrance was provided with additional glass canopies and lighting. The renovation gave the project a unified appearance, evoking the spirit of the great department stores of the turn of the century.

PROJECT FACTS

Address: Rue Neuve, rue de la Blanchisserie, rue des Cendres, Boulevard Botanique, 1000 Brussels, Belgium. **Client:** Citymo (Fortis Real Estate Group). **Period of construction:** 1998–1999. **Gross floor area:** 27,000 m². **Estimated visitors:** approx. 50,000 per day. **Additional functions:** offices, residential. **Co-interior architects:** Agence Design Architectural. **Structural engineering:** Setesco. **Original building:** Aaron Chelouche, Lathrop-Douglass, Marie-Bernadette Raimbault (1978).

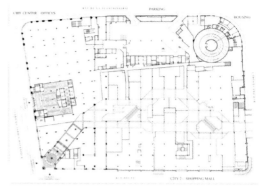

←← | "La ville dans la ville", lithography by
François Schuiten
↗ | Side elevation view
→ | Front façade
↑ | Ground floor plan
↓ | Isometry

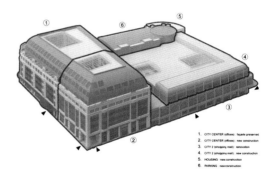

1. CITY CENTER (offices) façade preserved
2. CITY CENTER (offices) new construction
3. CITY 2 (shopping mall) renovation
4. CITY 2 (shopping mall) new construction
5. HOUSING new construction
6. PARKING new construction

↑ | Interior
↗ | Exterior
→ | Atrium

Arena Mall
Dubai Sports City

Dubai Sports City is the world's first purpose-built sports city and part of the Dubailand development in the desert. As the largest retail destination in Dubai Sports City, the Arena Mall will attract the 70,000 individuals residing and working within the development for shopping, dining and entertainment on a regular basis. The mall is situated in the heart of the stadium district, surrounded by four stadiums built by gmp. Presenting some 230 retail outlets, the mall's diverse retail mix will provide an appealing combination of specialty stores, everyday shopping outlets and unique sporting and lifestyle products. Situated on Emirates Road, the Arena Mall is perfectly positioned to serve the growing needs of the surrounding population, which represents one of the most intensively developed regions in the Middle East.

Address: Emirates Road, Dubailand, Dubai, United Arab Emirates. **Client:** Dubai Sports City. **Completion:** 2009. **Gross floor area:** 130,200 m². **Estimated visitors:** approx. 50,000 per day.

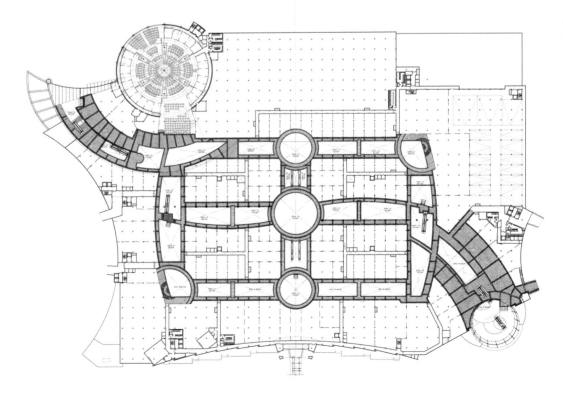

↑ | **Aerial**
← | **Floor plan paving**

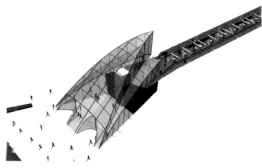

← | **Interior**
↑ | **Conceptual sketch,** bridge
↓ | **Dealership entrance**

↑ | Square

MALL Q19

Vienna

The historic, listed Samum paper factory in Vienna's 19th municipal quarter is an early example of a structure built using a reinforced concrete framework (by P. J. Manz, 1909). The juxtaposition of this building to the newly built structure gives rise to a new neighborhood called Q19, which thrives on this tension between new and old. Executed in cast-in-place concrete, the addition consists of two shopping levels, two underground garages and four levels of parking above – fitting in a total of 635 cars. The space between the old and new buildings is inhabited by a steel structure supporting a glass skin. On the one hand, this addition clearly separates the buildings, while on the other an interesting spatial experience is simultaneously created. The square situated in front of the shopping center connects with the northern section of Kreil square to result in a single public area. The section of the new building's façade facing the square above the main entrance is covered with aluminum lamellae acting as sun protectors.

PROJECT FACTS

Address: Kreilplatz 1, 1190 Vienna, Austria. **Client:** DHP Immobilien Leasing GmbH. **Period of planning:** 1999–2005. **Period of construction:** 2003–2005. **Gross floor area:** 54,366 m². **Additional functions:** offices, fitness center, parking. **Structural engineering:** werkraum.

↑↓ | **Interior**
↙ | **Parking**

↑ | Interior
← | Exterior

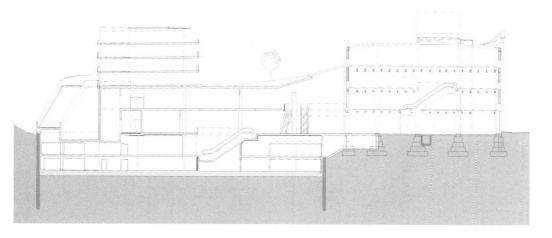

↖ | Section
← | Floor plan
↓ | Parking

↑ | **Department store entrance**
→ | **Atrium,** crossing escalators

Kamppi Commercial Center
Helsinki

The cityscape of the new Kamppi district is conversing with the basic functional idea. Facing Mannerheimintie Street, the department store expresses the main operating theme using brick-dominated city center mosaic. The commercial spaces complement the service range of the city center and improve its competitiveness compared with other commercial hubs nearby. The interior space represents the 21st Century, where the choice of materials is ruled by lifespan philosophy: they are aesthetic, functional, technically durable and economical now and in the future. A functional context takes on the main role through the wide removable glass walls and lighting that utilizes the latest technology.

PROJECT FACTS

Address: Urho Kekkosen katu 5 A, Helsinki, Finland. **Client:** Limited company SRV Viitoset Oy, Helsinki City Real Estate Department, Helsinki Kamppi Center Ltd. **Completion:** 2006. **Gross floor area:** 131,300 m². **Additional functions:** offices, housing, three public transport terminals. **Architects public outdoor areas:** Juhani Pallasmaa Architects.

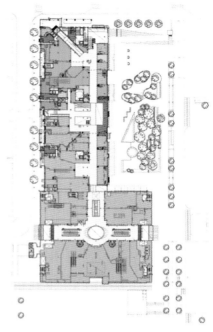

←←| Tennispalatsi square, dwelling houses
← | Aerial view from east
↑ | Floor plan
↓ | Department store and Narinkka square

Ehrenkrantz Eckstut & Kuhn,
EE&K

↑ | Exterior
↗ | Aerial
↗↗ | Kodak Theater
→ | Courtyard
→→| Stair aerial

Hollywood & Highland
Los Angeles

The new home of the Academy Awards, the Kodak Theater, incorporates both historical and legendary elements of the heyday of Hollywood Boulevard. The development includes retail, entertainment and residential components. The principal goal was to revive
the original pedestrian-friendly streetscape and to create restrained façades that respond
to the rhythm, massing, signage and ornamentation of early 20th Century adjacent buildings. Inside the project's precincts, visitors experience a series of forecourts and outdoor
stages, linked by distinctive promenades. To maintain the pedestrian character of the
boulevard, the vehicular entrance is located on a side street, through a courtyard landscaped as an orange grove.

PROJECT FACTS

Address: 6801 Hollywood Boulevard, Los Angeles, CA 90028, USA. **Client:** Trizec Hahn. **Completion:** 2001. **Gross floor area:** 120,780 m². **Estimated visitors:** approx. 75,000 per day. **Additional functions:** gathering spaces, television broadcast facilities, bowling alley, cinema, theater, nightclub. **Co-architects:** Altoon and Porter and others. **Landscape designer:** Rios Associates. **Interior designer:** Cole Martinez Curtis & Associates. **Lighting designer:** Lighting Design Alliance – LA.

LEGEND
- RETAIL/FASHION
- STUDIOS
- RESTAURANTS
- MUSIC
- PREMIERE THEATER
- CINEMA
- BALLROOM
- HOTEL
- WALKWAYS
- PARKING
- SERVICE

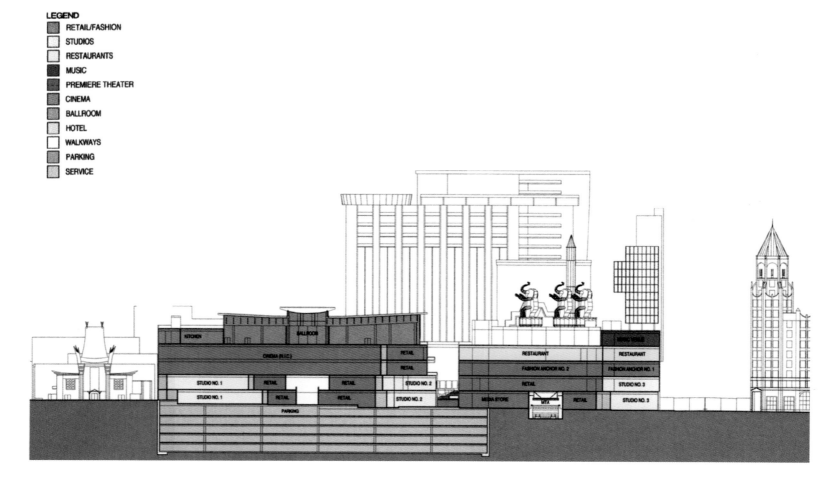

←←| **Corners**
↙↙| **Elevation**
←| **Drawing**
↓| **Plan**

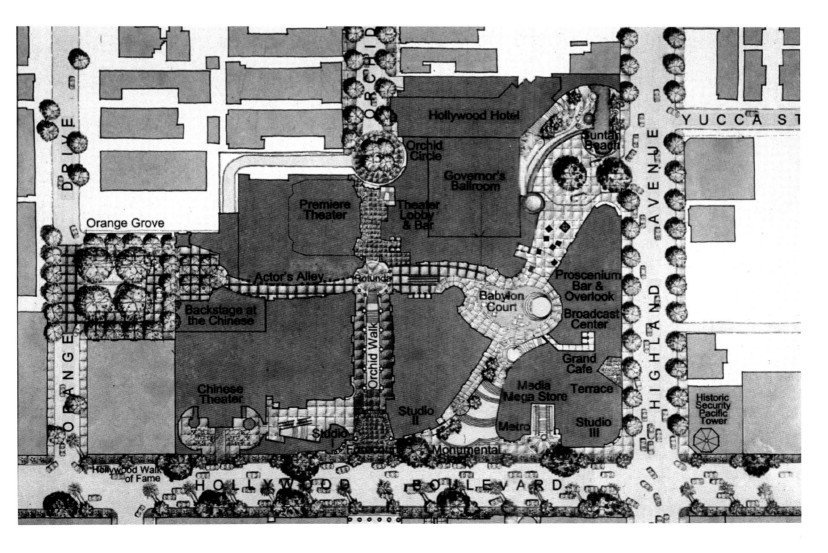

↑ | **Exterior**
→ | **Interior**

Peek & Cloppenburg department store
Mannheim

The Word City House Peek & Cloppenburg is a clear cube resting on beams with a steel-and-glass façade that lets plentiful light into the sales spaces. True to its "Light is life" motto, Richard Meier has created a transparent cuboid that radiates openness and allows an unrestricted view of the surrounding urban life. Glass, white aluminum panels, light natural stone and oak parquet define the elegant structure, whose geometry reflects the right-angled geometry of Mannheim's center. Thus, Roman travertine creates a strong contrast to the glass surfaces of the façade stretching the height of four floors.

Address: O3, 2–3, 68161 Mannheim, Germany. **Client:** Peek & Cloppenburg. **Period of construction:** 2005–2007. **Gross floor area:** 18,500 m². **Light design:** netvico GmbH.

—←| **Façade,** inside
—↓| **Interior**

↑ | **Interior Canyon,** carefully sculpted path with
variety of bridges, coves and other exploratory spaces
→ | **Aerial**

Namba Parks
Osaka

Namba Parks inserts a much-needed natural amenity into the dense city core. Located
next to Namba Train Station, it is a key gateway project for Osaka in terms of redefin-
ing the city's identity. The canyon, constructed from bands of colored stone, reinforces
the project's connection with nature while forming Jerde primary circulation pattern with
a variety of coves, caves, valleys, outdoor terraces and other exploratory spaces. Glass
bridges connect the two sides of the canyon, by night becoming arching tubes of light. By
connecting to the street, the sloping park plane will draw people up and into the project.
Namba Parks' retail and entertainment venues are accessed through a figure-eight circulation path that ascends through the canyon interior up the sloped park plane.

PROJECT FACTS

Address: Namba 5-chome, Namba, Japan. **Client:** Nankai Electric Co., Ltd., Obayashi Corporation. **Completion:** 2003. **Gross floor area:** 130,000 m². **Estimated visitors:** approx. 43,500 per day. **Additional functions:** office, cultural, entertainment. **Landscape architect:** EDAW, Inc.

↑ | **Rooftop park,** with groves of trees, lawn,
water features and other natural amenities
← | **Man-made canyon,** constructed from bands
of colored stone

← | **Aerial,** view from the office tower
↓ | **Site plan,** phase 1

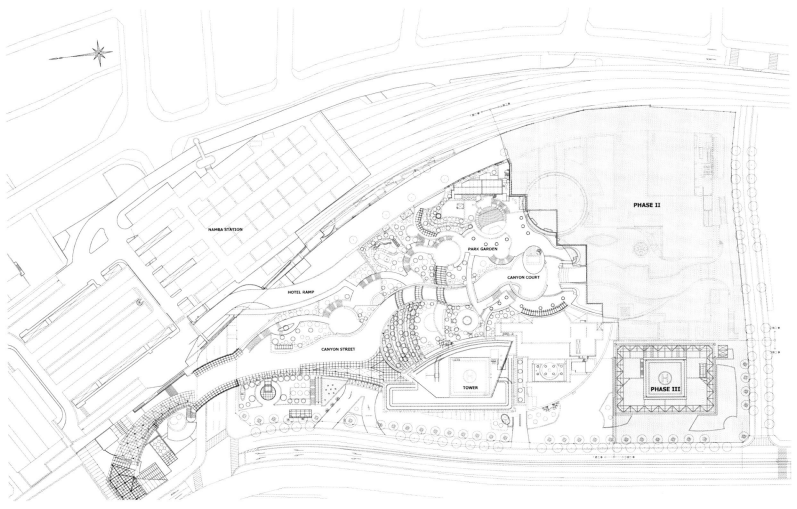

José Manuel Quintela da Fonseca

↑ | **Exterior**
→ | **Interior,** detail

ALEXA

Berlin

East Berlin's largest shopping center is located on one of the last city hubs still undergoing development – Alexanderplatz. The architecture plays with the motifs from the roaring twenties with its art deco elements, recalling a mythical period for the metropolis on the Spree. The forms are not simply copied, but varied and amplified. The structure of the façade with an enlarged rounded arch frieze acts on the art deco principle of motif repetition and variation of architectonic vocabulary, simultaneously creating a counterpart to the neighboring arches of the elevated train viaduct. The volume is externally separated into individual building volumes, while inside a comprehensive circulation concept unites the entire space.

PROJECT FACTS

Address: Alexanderplatz 4, 10178 Berlin, Germany. **Client:** Sierra Fund / Foncière Euris. **Period of construction:** 2004–2007. **Gross floor area:** 56,200 m². **Additional functions:** childrens edutainment center, model railway world. **Development:** Sonae Sierra / Foncière Euris.

←← | **Interior,** balconies
← | **Detail decoration**
↙ | **Mall,** levels
↓ | **Floor decoration**

↑ | **Courtyard**
→ | **Entry**

Paseo Colorado

Pasadena

In order to revitalize a three-block shopping mall along Colorado Boulevard in downtown Pasadena, Edward Bennet's 1923 Beaux-Arts plan for the civic center district was consulted. The existing mall had cut off the adjacent Garfield Avenue and interrupted the intended view corridor between the Civic Auditorium and the historic Public Library. This central axis was restored by creating the Garfield Promenade, where pedestrians can window shop and enjoy the outdoors. Paseo Colorado branches off across from the new Garfield Court, complementing the open air area with its roofed-over space. Changes in plan geometry, staircases, sculptural elements and elevations emphasize different views. The mall is not just an isolated project, but is part of a district-wide plan.

PROJECT FACTS

Address: 280 East Colorado Boulevard, Pasadena, California 91101, USA. **Client:** Trizec Hahn. **Completion:** 2001. **Gross floor area:** 5,200 m². **Additional functions:** residential, movie theater, fitness center. **Landscape architect:** Melendrez Design Partners.

↑ | **Entrance**
← | **Courtyard**

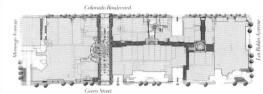

⊣ Streetwall corner
∠ Courtyard
↑ Site plan
↓ Plan

↑ | **Intimates,** with seating group, stylized floral motifs and nude silhouettes are on the hall
→ | **Atrium,** skylight with mobile created by sculptor Brandon d'Leo

Bloomingdale's
Chevy Chase

The three-level store is located in Wisconsin Place Center which is at the border of Washington DC. The main floor is one level above the open plaza. The store continues to demonstrate Bloomingdale's merchandise mix, which emphasizes designer and luxury brands. The design is quite contemporary and continues to pursue variations on the signature "black & white" image of the 59th street flagship in New York City. The new store features a 40-foot circular atrium topped by a skylight. Glass-enclosed escalators traverse the atrium and enhance the sightlines to all the sales floors. There are four three-storied black glass clad columns that punctuate this atrium. Black granite and black mirrors are used generously to accent the space and as architectural icons.

PROJECT FACTS

Address: 5300 Western Avenue, Chevy Chase, MD 20815, Maryland, USA. **Client:** Bloomingdale's. **Completion:** 2007. **Gross floor area:** 16,950 m². **Architect of record:** Krell Corcoran Associates PC. **Lighting consultant:** HLB Lighting.

←←| **The Home Store,** with bleached bamboo
floors, black lacquer and chocolate accents
↙ **Visual presentation,** with two classifica-
tions: Casual / Contemporary and Formal / Traditional
← **The New View,** with either black mirror,
lacquer or marble
↓ **Customer Service,** in the mood of interior
decorator Dorothy Draper, who popularized
the "Hollywood Regency" style in the 1930's

←← | **Women's shoe collections,** polished chrome table, a custom design of Mancini Duffy
← **Alcove table,** projecting a mother-of-pearl finish with Kinon and a silver-leafed wall covering
↓ **Women's shoe collections,** appointed with residential furnishings and punctuated by over-scaled beveled mirrors

tects

Index

Altoon + Porter Architects, LLP

444 South Flower Street, 48th Floor
Los Angeles, CA 90071 (USA)
T +1. 213.2251900
F +1 213.2251901
scervantes@altoonporter.com
www.altoonporter.com

→ **210**

Tadao Ando Architect & Associates

5-23 Toyosaki 2-Chome Kita-ku
531–0072 Osaka (Japan)
T +81.6.63751148
F +81.6.63746240
taaa@diary.ocn.ne.jp

→ **154**

Atelier d'Art Urbain

7 Avenue Lloyd George
1000 Brussels (Belgium)
T +32.2.3446464
F +32.2.3463600
mail@atelier-art-urbain.com
www.atelier-art-urbain.com

→ **372**

au4g

7, Impasse Charles Petit
75011 Paris (France)
T +33.1.43568440
F +33.1.34562242
au4g@wanadoo.fr
www.au4g.fr

→ **278, 296**

Sabri Bendimérad, architect

c/o tectône
29, rue Traversière
75 012 Paris (France)
T +33.1.40020303
F +33.1.40020307
sabri.b@wanadoo.fr
www.tectone.net

→ **114**

Burckhardt + Partner

Galgenfeldweg 16
3000 Berne 22 (Switzerland)
T +41.31.3352111
T +41.31.3352155
bern@burckhardtpartner.ch
www.burckhardtpartner.ch

→ **30**

BRT Architekten

Oberbaumbrücke 1
20457 Hamburg (Germany)
T +49.40.248420
F +49.40.24842222
office@brt.de
www.brt.de

→ **242**

Tuncer Cakmakli Architects

Galip dede cad. Yoruk Cikmazi 8
34420 Beyoglu / Istanbul (Turkey)
T +90.212.2492164
F +90.212.2492295
info@cakmakli.com
www.cakmakli.com

→ **60**

Chapman Taylor Architetti Milan

Piazzetta Pattari 1
20122 Milan (Italy)
T +39.02.89095077
F +39.02.72080799
architetti@chapmantaylor.it
www.chapmantaylor.it

→ **136, 256**

Chapman Taylor

Goya, 4 2ª Planta
28001 Madrid (Spain)
T +34.91.4170925
F +34.91.4170926
ctesp@chapmantaylor.es
www.chapmantaylor.com

→ **70, 84, 190**

Chapman Taylor

96 Kensington High Street
London W8 4SG (United Kingdom)
T +44.20.73713000
F +44.20.73711949
ctlondon@chapmantaylor.com
www.chapmantaylor.com

→ **234**

Chetwood Associates

12-13 Clerkenwell Green
London EC1R 0QJ (United Kingdom)
T +44.20.74902400
F +44.20.72501916
laurie.chetwood@chetwoods-london.com
www.chetwoods.com

→ **186**

pierfrancesco Cravel pfcarchitects

via Giangiacomo Mora, 7
20100 Milan (Italy)
T +39.02.36520367
F +39.02.99988190
info@pfcarchitects.com
www.pfcarchitects.com

→ 48

José Guedes Cruz

Rua Monte Olivete 53
1200–279 Lisbon (Portugal)
T +351.21.3977845
F +351.21.3977938
atelier@guedescruz.com
www.guedescruz.com

→ 260

de Architekten Cie.

Keizersgracht 126
1015 CW Amsterdam (The Netherlands)
T +31.20.5309300
F +31.20.5309399
r.v.d.linde@cie.nl
www.cie.nl

→ 244, 308

Design 103 International

9th Floor, Asoke Towers Office Building
219/24,28-31 Asoke Road
Sukhumvit 21 Klongtoey Nuea
Klongtoey Bangkok 10110 (Thailand)
www.d103group.com

→ 332

Despang Architekten

Am Graswege 5
30169 Hanover (Germany)
T +49.511.882840
F +49.511.887985
info@despangarchitekten.de

College of Architecture
University of Nebraska-Lincoln
238 Architecture Hall West
P. O. Box 880107
Lincoln NE 68588-0107 (USA)
T +1.402.4729956
F +1.402.4723806
mdespang2@unl.edu
www.despangarchitekten.de

→ 166

Lena Pessoa / DeuxL

9, rue de Normandie
75003 Paris (France)
T +33.1.42418750
F +33.1.42418752
contact@deuxl.com
www.deuxl.com

→ 362

Dougall Design Associates, Inc., interior designers

35 North Arroyo Parkway, suite 200
Pasadena, CA 91103 (USA)
T +1.626.4326464
F +1.626.4326460
dda@dougalldesign.com
www.dougalldesign.com

→ 274

(EEA) Erick van Egeraat

Calandstraat 2
3016 CA Rotterdam (The Netherlands)
T +31.10.4369686
F +31.10.4369573
eea.l@eea-architects.com
www.eea-architects.com

→ 354

Ehrenkrantz Eckstut & Kuhn, EE&K

162 Avenue of the Americas 3rd Floor,
New York, NY 10013 (USA)
T +1.212.3530400
F +1.212.2283928
tcorabella@eekarchitects.com
www.eekarchitects.com

→ 88, 404

Elkus Manfredi Architects

300 A Street,
Boston, MA 02210 (USA)
T +1.617.4261300
F +1.617.4267502
tcoulard@elkus-manfredi.com
www.elkus-manfredi.com

→ 18

ELS Architecture and Urban Design

2040 Addison Street
Berkeley, CA 94704 (USA)
T +1.510.5492929
F +1.510.8433304
rusin@elsarch.com
www.elsarch.com

→ 350

F+A Architects

117 East Colorado Boulevard, Fifth Floor
Pasadena, CA 91105 (USA)
T +1.626.3512500
F +1.626.3512512
info@faarchitects.com
www.faarchitects.com

→ 40, 66, 376

Fitch Design PTE LTD

121–141 Westbourne Terrace
London W2 6JR (United Kingdom)
T +44.20.74790223
F +44.20.74790340
Brendan.mcknight@fitch.com
www.fitch.com

→ 170

Foreign Office Architects

55 Curtain Road
EC2A 3PT London (United Kingdom)
T +44.20.70339800
F +44.20.70339801
london@f-o-a.net
www.f-o-a.net

→ 36

Massimiliano Fuksas

Piazza del Monte di Pietà 30
00186 Rome (Italy)
T +39.06.68807871
F +39.06.68807872
fuksaspublications@fuksas.it
www.fuksas.it

→ 52

Future Systems

The Warehouse, 20 Victoria Gardens
London W11 3PE (United Kingdom)
T +44.20.72437670
F +44.20.72437690
email@future-systems.com
www.future-systems.com

→ 220

Grimshaw

57 Clerkenwell Road
London EC1M 5NG (United Kingdom)
T +44.20.7291.4141
F +44.20.7291.4194
info@grimshaw-architects.com
www.grimshaw-architects.com

→ 148

Haskoll architects

39 Harrington Gardens
London SW7 4JU (United Kingdom)
T +44.20.78351188
F +44.20.73737230
info@haskoll.co.uk
www.haskoll.co.uk

→ 312

Helin & Co Architects

Urho Kekkosen katu 3 B, P.O.Box 1333
00101 Helsinki (Finland)
T +358.207.577808
F +358.207.577801
info@helinco.fi
www.helinco.fi

→ 202, 384

Holzer Kobler Architekturen

Ankerstrasse 3
8004 Zurich (Switzerland)
T +41.44.2405200
F +41.44.2405202
mail@holzerkobler.ch
www.holzerkobler.ch

→ 44, 106

HYDEA srl

Via del Rosso Fiorentino, 2/G
50142 Florence (Italy)
T +39.055.719491
F +39.055.7135233
mail@hydea.it
www.hydea.com

→ 26, 140

Toyo Ito & Associates, Architects

Fujiya Bldg. 19-4 1-Chome, Shibuya, Shibuya-ku
150-0002 Tokyo (Japan)
T +81.3.34095822
info@toyo-ito.co.jp
www.toyo-ito.co.jp

→ 172

The Jerde Partnership

913 Ocean Front Walk
Venice, CA 90291 (USA)
T +1.310.3991987
F +1.310.3921316
www.jerde.com

→ 102, 324, 340, 346, 396

JRDV Architects

827 Broadway, Suite 300
Oakland, CA 94607 (USA)
T +1.510.2954395
F +1.510.8351984
anna@jrdv.com
www.jrdv.com

→ 32, 56

k4 architects, Vladimír Pacek

Kocianka 8/10
612 00 Brno (Czech Republic)
T +420.542.216753
F +420.542.216750
brno@k4.cz
www.k4.cz

→ 22

Louis Karol

The Palms, 2nd Floor
145 Sir Lowry Road
Cape Town 8001 (South Africa)
T +27.21.4624500
F +27.21.4624550
info@louiskarol.com
www. louiskarol.com

→ 360

Josef Paul Kleihues, Kleihues + Kleihues

Helmholtzstraße 42
10587 Berlin (Germany)
T +49.30.3997790
F +49.30.39977977
berlin@kleihues.com
www.kleihues.com

→ 252, 328

Klein Dytham architecture (KDa)

AD Building 2F 1-15-7 Hiroo, Shibuya-ku
Tokyo 150-0012 (Japan)
T +81.3.57952277
F +81.3.57952276
kda@klein-dytham.com
www.klein-dytham.com

→ 316, 336

Eric R Kuhne & Associates

15-27 Gee Street, Clerkenwell
London EC1V 3RD (United Kingdom)
T +44.20.7549 8499
F +44.20.7549 8449
enquiries@civicart.com
www.civicart.com

→ 80

Léon Wohlhage Wernik Architekten

Leibnizstraße 65
10629 Berlin (Germany)
T +49.30.3276000
F +49.30.32760060
post@leonwohlhagewernik.de
www.leonwohlhagewernik.de

→ 120

Studio Daniel Libeskind

2 Rector Street, 19th Floor
New York, NY 10006 (USA)
T +1.212.4979100
F +1.212.2852130
info@daniel-libeskind.com
www.daniel-libeskind.com

→ 20

Mancini Duffy

39 West 13th Street
New York, NY 10011 (USA)
T +1.212.9381260
+1.212.9381267
pleiweiss@manciniduffy.com
www.manciniduffy.com

→ 408

Mei Architecten en stedenbouwers

Jobsveem, Lloydstraat 138
3024 EA Rotterdam (The Netherlands)
T +31.10.4252222
F +31.10.4781300
info@mei-arch.nl
www.mei-arch.nl

→ 270

Richard Meier

475 Tenth Avenue, 6th Floor
New York, NY 10018 (USA)
T +1.212.9676060
F +1.212.9673207
mail@richardmeier.com
www.richardmeier.com

→ 392

C. F. Møller Architects

Europaplads 2
11. 8000 Århus C (Denmark)
T +45.8730.5300
F +45.8730.5399
cfmoller@cfmoller.com
www.cfmoller.com

→ 122

Musson Cattell Mackey Partnership

1600 – Two Bentall Centre, 555 Burrard Street
Box 264
Vancouver, BC V7X 1M9 (Canada)
T +1.604.6872990
F +1.604.6871771
mcmp@mcmparchitects.com
www.mcmparchitects.com

→ 40

NÄGELIARCHITEKTEN
architectural office

Lychener Straße 43
10435 Berlin (Germany)
T +49.30.61609712
F +49.30.61609714
buero@naegeliarchitekten.de
www.naegeliarchitekten.de

→ 194

Jean Nouvel

10 Cité d'Angoulême
75011 Paris (France)
T +33.1.49238383
F +33.1.43148110
info@jeannouvel.fr
www.jeannouvel.com

→ 298, 358

OIII

Grasweg 79
1031 HX Amsterdam (The Netherlands)
T +31.20.6277140
F +31.20.6251804
info@o-drie.nl
www.o-drie.nl

→ 130

Omniplan

1845 Woodall Rodgers Freeway Ste. 1500
Dallas, TX 75201 (USA)
T +1.214.7756181
F +1.214.8267016
cwalls@omniplan.com
www.omniplan.com

→ 12

Pei, Cobb, Freed & Partners

88 Pine Street
New York, NY 10005 (USA)
T +1.212.7513122
F +1.212.8725443
pcf@pcf-p.com
www.pcf-p.com

→ 298

Renzo Piano Building Workshop

Via Rubens 29
16158 Genoa (Italy)
T +39.010.61711
F +39.010.6171350
italy@rpbw.com
www. rpbw.com

→ 366

peterlorenzateliers

Maria Theresien Straße 37
6020 Innsbruck (Austria)
T +43.512.586845
F +43.512.561893

Kreilplatz 1/3
1190 Vienna (Austria)
T +43.1.5334908
F +43.1.533490817
office@peterlorenz.at
www.peterlorenz.at

→ 212, 380

Christian de Portzamparc

1, rue de l'Aude
75014 Paris (France)
T +33.1.40648005
F +33.1.43277479
studio@chdeportzamparc.com
www.chdeportzamparc.com

→ 226

PSP Pysall Stahrenberg & Partner

Lietzenburger Straße 44
10789 Berlin (Germany)
T +49.30.2308430
F +49.30.23084388
mail@arch-psp-berlin.de
www.psp-architekten.de

→ 264

José Manuel Quintela da Fonseca

Rua Amílcar Cabral, 23
1750–018 Lisbon (Portugal)
T +351.21.7515000
F +351.21.7582688
www.sonaesierra.com

→ 76, 198, 400

Riehle + Partner

Dominohaus
Am Echazufer 24
72764 Reutlingen (Germany)
T +49.7121.9270
F +49.7121.927200
mail@riehle-partner.de
www.riehle-partner.de

→ 96

RKW Rhode Kellermann Wawrowsky Architektur + Städtebau

Büro Düsseldorf
Tersteegenstraße 30
40474 Düsseldorf (Germany)
T +49.0211.43670
F +49.0211.4367111
info@rkwmail.de
www.rkw-as.de

→ 118, 238, 248, 290

RTKL Associates Inc.

901 South Bond Street
Baltimore, MD 21231 (USA)
T +1.410.5376000
F +1.410.2762136
Baltimore-Info@rtkl.com
www.rtkl.com

→ 144, 150, 286, 320, 332

Hans Ruijssenaars Architecten

Barentszplein 7
1013 NJ Amsterdam (The Netherlands)
T +31.20.5304830
F +31.20.5304838
info@ruijssenaars.nl
www.ruijssenaars.nl

→ 268

SMC Alsop Architects

Parkgate Studio, 41 Parkgate Road
London SW11 4NP (United Kingdom)
T +44.20.7978 7878
F +44.20.7978 7879
info@smcalsop.com
www.smcalsop.com

→ 294, 304

Snøhetta

Skur 39, Vippetangen
0150 Oslo (Norway)
T +47.24.15606
F +47.24.156061
contact@snoarc.no
www.snoarc.no

→ 64

Sua Kay Architects

Rua D. Luís I, nº 3–5º
1200–149 Lisbon (Portugal)
T +351.21.3931960
F –351.21.3902930
suakay@suakay.com
www.suakay.com

→ 206

Suttle Mindlin

345 Marshall Avenue, Suite 102
St. Louis, MO 63119 (USA)
T +1.314.9610102
F +1.314.9610139
mmindlin@suttle-mindlin.com
www.suttle-mindlin.com

→ 162

Sergei Tchoban nps tchoban voss GbR Architekten BDA, A. M. Prasch P. Sigl S. Tchoban E. Voss

Rosenthaler Straße 40/41
10178 Berlin (Germany)
T +49.30.2839200
F +49.30.283920200
berlin@npstv.de
www.npstv.de

→ 92, 282

Thompson, Ventulett, Stainback & Associates

2700 Promenade Two, 1230 Peachtree Street NE,
Atlanta, GA 30309 (USA)
T +1.404.9466600
F +1.404.6826700
architecture@tvsa.com
www.tvsa.com

→ 158

Oswald Matthias Ungers

Belvederestraße 60
50933 Cologne (Germany)
T +49.221.9498360
F +49.221.9498366
koeln@omungers.de
www.omungers.de

→ 298

UNStudio

Stadhouderskade 113
1070 AJ Amsterdam (The Nether ands)
T +31.20.5702040
F +31.20.5702041
info@unstudio.com
www.unstudio.com

→ 230, 344

Valode & Pistre

115, rue du Bac
75007 Paris (France)
T +33.1.5363 2200
F +33.1.53632209
info@v-p.com
www.valode-et-pistre.com

→ 132

Vasconi Associés Architectes

58 rue Monsieur Le Prince
75006 Paris (France)
T +33.1.53737475
F +33.1.53737450
agence@claude-vasconi.fr
www.claude-vasconi.fr

→ 110

A & D Wejchert & Partners, Architects

23 Lower Baggot Street
Dublin 2 (Ireland)
T +353.1.6610321
F +353.1.6610203
mail@wejchert.ie
www.wejchert.ie

→ 126

Zeidler Partnership Architects

Room 703, Hyundai Motor Tower, No. 38 Xiaoyun Road
Chaoyang, Beijing 100027 (China)
T +86.10.8453 9828 ext. 819
F +86.10.8453 9838
shou@zpa.net.cn
www.zpa.net.cn

→ 176

All other pictures, portraits and plans were made availa-
ble by the architects.

Cover:
front side: Gardette, Grégoire
back side: Davies, Richard (l.),
Scagliola & Partners (r.)

IMPRINT

The Deutsche Bibliothek is registering this publication in the Deutsche Nationalbibliographie; detailed bibliographical information can be found on the Internet at http://dnb.ddb.de

ISBN 978-3-938780-27-5

© 2008 by Verlagshaus Braun
www.verlagshaus-braun.de

1st edition 2008

Editorial staff: Annika Schulz
Draft texts by the architects.
Text editing: Chris van Uffelen
Translation: Alice Bayandin
Graphic concept: ON Grafik, Hamburg
Layout: Georgia van Uffelen
Reproduction: Bild1Druck GmbH, Berlin